3-1-22

Dear Faith & Bart,

Merry christmas &
a Happy New Year from
all of us "down under".

love Denise, Andrew,
Lachlan & Olivia.

25.12.94.

AUSTRALIA
THE BEAUTIFUL LAND

AUSTRALIA

THE BEAUTIFUL LAND

NATIONAL
BOOK DISTRIBUTORS
AND PUBLISHERS

Published by National Book Distributors and Publishers Pty Ltd
Unit 3/2 Aquatic Drive, Frenchs Forest, NSW, Australia, 2086

First edition 1994
Text © Bruce Elder
Photographs © individual photographers and/or their agents as follows:

R Barnett: pages 10; 13; 30; 32 (bottom); 33; 36-41; 44; 46; 48; 57 (top); 58; 60-61; 91; 94; 112; 114-116; 118-121; 124-125 **W Darran Leal**: page 82 (Auscape International) **N Rains**: pages 2-3 (title page); 14; 26; 28-29; 32 (top); 34-35; 42-43; 45 (bottom right); 47; 49; 50-52; 53 (top – APL); 54-56; 57 (bottom); 59 (APL); 64; 68-81; 86; 89 (top and bottom right); 90; 92-93; 95 (bottom); 96-111; 122-123; 126-128; 130-131; 136; 140; 144-167 **P Steel**: pages 15-16; 19; 25; 62-63 (top); 66 (top); 67; 84-85; 88; 117; 138-139 **K Stepnell**: pages 20; 63 (bottom); 66 (bottom); 132-135; 137; 142; 143 **Struik Image Library**: cover; frontispiece; pages 5; 6; 11; 23; 168

Designer Neville Poulter
Design assistant Lyndall Hamilton
Editor Annlerie van Rooyen
Editorial assistant Jenny Barrett
Cartographer Loretta Chegwidden

Reproduction by Unifoto (Pty) Ltd, Cape Town
Printed and bound by Kyodo Printing Company (Pte) Ltd, Singapore

National Library of Australia
Cataloguing-in-Publication data
Elder, Bruce
Australia the Beautiful Land

ISBN 1 86436 004 6

The combination of a modern highrise central business district and one of the most beautiful natural harbours in the world ensures that Sydney becomes a wonderland of water and lights at night. The Opera House and the Harbour Bridge are illuminated and Centrepoint tower, the highest building in the city, stands like a sentinel (frontispiece).
Green Island (previous pages), a remarkable coral island in the northern section of the Great Barrier Reef, has long been one of Cairns' prime tourist attractions. A small, uninhabited island, it once had nothing more than a jetty with a marine viewing point at the end. In recent times a resort has been established on the island and it has a Marineland, a Barrier Reef Theatre, a variety of snorkelling trails and several eating facilities.
Although regarded as a hot, dry continent in winter, the Australian Alps, which stretch from southern New South Wales to northern Victoria, are frequently covered with snow. They attract skiers from all over the world to alpine resorts like Perisher Valley (right) and Smiggin Holes.
One of the delights of Adelaide, particularly after a hot summer's day, is a stroll beside Torrens Lake at sunset. The European history of the city is captured by the English trees beside the river and the graceful band rotunda in Elder Park (next page) just below the city's Festival Centre.

CONTENTS

THE LIE OF THE LAND

AUSTRALIA IS AT ONCE THE WORLD'S SMALLEST continent and largest island; it is said that it is also the oldest continent, weathered flat by the unrelenting forces of nature over millions of years. Whichever way Australia is seen, it is unlike any other place on Earth.

There is no better way to understand the lie of this vast land than to stand at Ellery Creek Big Hole, one of the many gorges and chasms which cut through the MacDonnell Mountain Ranges to the west of Alice Springs. Above the waterhole is a cliff face twisted into peculiar shapes, the bedding resembling a piece of putty crushed by some Dreamtime giant. A notice board near the car park explains: 'All around you there is evidence of a great mountain-building episode in the formation of Central Australia. You can see tortured folds of rock which formed deep in the earth ... great heat and pressure pushed up 10,000-metre mountains but 350 million years of erosion have almost worn them away, exposing the deeper folded rocks. These rocks were formed from mud and sand which were deposited as flat layers on the bed of an inland sea.'

That a mountain range higher than the Himalayas was worn away by 350 million years of erosion demonstrates the way the continent has developed. Even if Australia is not the oldest continent, it certainly is the flattest with only six per cent of the land higher than 700 metres. The country's highest mountain, Mount Kosciusko, is only 2,229 metres above sea level — scarcely more than a substantial hill!

The physical shape of Australia can best be explained in terms of five distinct regions. Along the east coast (the most densely populated area in the country) is a narrow coastal plain nestling between the Pacific Ocean and the Great Dividing Range. Consisting of a series of low hills, plateaux, high plains and, in some places, spectacular gorges, The Great Dividing Range runs from northern Queensland to the southern tip of Tasmania. These two regions are the country's most productive land, blessed with fertile soils and enjoying both good rainfall and moderate temperatures.

Beyond the Great Dividing Range are the Murray, Eyre and Carpentaria basins which stretch from the Gulf of Carpentaria down through western Queensland and New South Wales, into western Victoria and South Australia. The early European explorers thought this region was an immense inland sea. All the major river systems run in a southwesterly direction, either reaching Lake Eyre (Australia's largest lake with a catchment area of some 1.3 million square kilometres) or joining the Murray-Darling river system and reaching the sea at Lake Alexandrina in South Australia.

More than half of Australia is taken up by the vast Western Shield, a series of low-lying plateaux and deserts extending from the Barkly Tableland in the Northern Territory across to the Western Australian coast. The Western Shield includes the extensive regions of the Great Victoria, Gibson and Great Sandy deserts — areas characterised by seemingly endless ridges of sand dunes and iron-rich red soils. This is where nature has weathered all the major formations to a point that only low-lying hills and remarkable rock outcrops such as Uluru (formerly Ayers Rock) and Kata Tjuta (the Olgas), the Devil's Marbles and the Bungle Bungles are left.

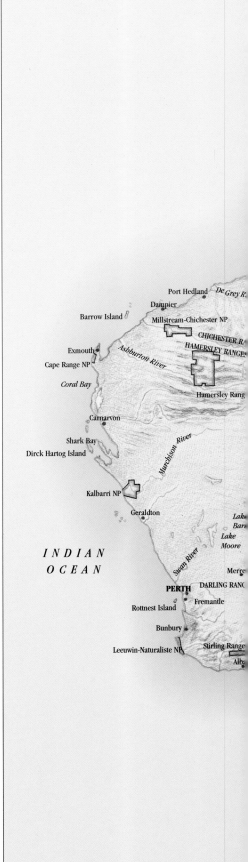

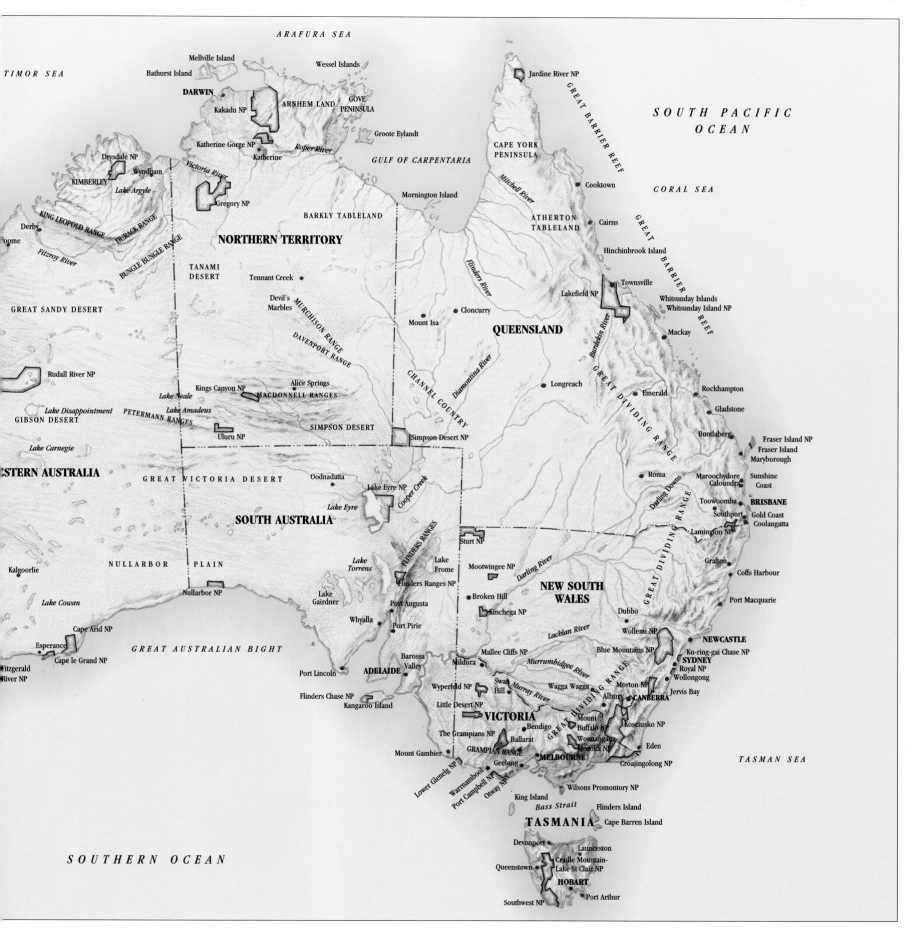

INTRODUCTION

Since the 1930s, the magnificent Sydney Harbour Bridge (opposite) has been the means by which people from Sydney's northern suburbs have reached the city centre.

Most of Australia's koalas live on the eastern coastal strip. There are a number of sanctuaries where visitors can watch these attractive animals in their natural habitat. The two koalas shown here (below) are residents of the Lone Pine Koala Sanctuary at Fig Tree Pocket in Queensland.

*S*ome 55,000 years ago, it has been estimated, when the sea level was 120 metres lower than it is today and the Australian continental landmass included both Tasmania and Papua New Guinea, the first humans reached Australia. These ancestors of modern-day Aborigines lived a peaceful, uncomplicated life as hunters and gatherers until 200 years ago, when a motley collection of criminals and their military wardens sailed up the east coast of Australia and, after a brief false start at Botany Bay, landed at Port Jackson.

On 26 January 1788, Captain Arthur Phillip stood on the shores of Sydney Cove, raised the British flag and took possession of half the continent in the name of the British king. The following day the convicts came ashore and began clearing the land where the modern city of Sydney would eventually grow.

From these unusual and oppressive beginnings, modern Australia evolved. Out of its convict past was forged a society with a genuine dislike of protocol and pretentiousness; a society where people's characters are measured by who they are rather than who their parents were or what they have achieved in life. Modern Australian society represents a repudiation of many of the deeply entrenched values of European society. It is a society where informality is important, where outdoor living and in recent times, an acceptance of change, have been embraced with ease.

The love of the outdoors, and the love of the sun which seems to shine down on much of the continent for much of the time, finds one of its most powerful manifestations in the weekend passion to head to the sports ovals or fields, either to watch or to participate. Whether people live in Sydney, Melbourne, Adelaide, Brisbane or Perth (and most Australians do), weekends are also there to escape to the magnificent beaches, to go bushwalking, surfing, fishing or just to breathe in some country air.

The famous Australian expatriate, Clive James, once declared that in Australia 'Life seemed very close to God' but worried that 'Paradise on Earth leaves you nothing to achieve'. In this sense Australia can make reasonable claims to being very close to the working class Utopia that the peoples of Europe have dreamt about for centuries. They think nothing of having a lifestyle which, in the nineteenth century, would have been reserved for the European aristocracy. Even after years of recession, most Australians still have high expectations — vacations on tropical islands, perhaps a holiday house on the coast, a couple of cars and an attractive home.

Possibly the greatest change experienced in recent times has been Australia's move towards multiculturalism. After World War II, over one million Europeans arrived in Australia, changing the predominantly English-speaking, Anglo-Saxon culture forever. The somewhat monotonous British cuisine — particularly the idea of meat and two vegetables at virtually every meal — gave way to international dishes. The pastas of Italy, the nouvelle cuisine of France, and the exotic fare of Southeast Asia all became an integral part of Australian society in the struggle to embrace people from different cultural and linguistic backgrounds.

Lately the acknowledgement of Asia's importance as one of the driving forces in the world economy has seen Australians turning their backs on their allegiance to Europe and recognising that, by dint of geographical reality, the country is closer to Asia. On the one hand the rapidly growing economies to the north are eager for Australian raw materials, and on the other Australians are eager to be part of the economic boom experienced in the whole of the Pacific basin.

*T*he site of the first landing in Australia is still the most important starting point for any exploration of the country. Famed worldwide for its distinctive Harbour Bridge and dramatic Opera House, Sydney, the one-time convict colony, is now the largest city in Australia. Its harbour, which so often sparkles in the harsh, southern sunlight, remains a source of amazement to visitors. As a city with a near-perfect climate, the sun shines for an average of 342 days a year. With evenly distributed rainfall, it experiences slightly more rain in the late autumn and early winter; glorious subtropical summer days of sunshine and soaring temperatures draw people to surfing and sun-bathing on the beaches north and south of The Heads at Sydney Harbour.

Sydney, particularly the leafy parklands around the harbour's foreshores, is a place of heady sensations, its smells of salt-water intermingled with the powerful fragrance of the frangipani. At night the skyline is a spectacle of lights, making the cityscape uniquely beautiful. The visitor need venture no further than the waterfront around the central business district to experience the charms of the city. The ferries from Circular Quay make their way to a kaleidoscope of attractive destinations around the harbour foreshores. The Opera House offers superb views across to Fort Denison and Government House, and Darling Harbour, a huge tourist development boasting gift shops, restaurants and hotels, is an entertaining retreat from the bustle of the city centre. Geologically, Sydney is a gigantic bowl, a huge saucer dipping in the middle and rising to the north, south and west. The sandstone plateaux at the edge of the basin have poor sandy soil, sustaining hardy native scrub which consist of stunted eucalypts, acacias and resilient small bushes.

With 3.7 million inhabitants, Sydney houses over 60 per cent of New South Wales' total population, but it does not account for the rich diversity of the rest of the state. Covering a total of 801,428 square kilometres (including Lord Howe Island), New South Wales is, as it likes to declare, 'The premier state' – apart from being the first place of European settlement, it is also the most industrialised and urbanised state in the Commonwealth. Part of the reason for this high urbanisation is the state's 1,900 kilometres of coastline. Combined with the seemingly universal desire to live beside the sea, it is hardly surprising that more than 90 per cent of the residents of New South Wales live within 20 kilometres of a beach. The coastal region is also one of great variety, ranging from the old river ports of Grafton and Maclean to the tumbling hills of the Great Dividing Range, so typical of the state's north coast. This area, which has become one of the country's centres of 'alternative lifestyles', is characterised by high rainfall, steamy days and a growth cycle which would make even the most inept city escapee into a successful farmer. Between the ridges of cultivation lie valleys of dense, subtropical rainforest with giant ferns, stinging trees and towering eucalypts.

The coastal plain between the Queensland border and the thriving city of Newcastle has some of the best agricultural land in the state. The rich alluvial soils of the plains – a result of the local rivers flooding in summer – combine with sunny days to produce an ideal environment for sugar cane, vegetables, bananas and more recently, macadamia nuts, avocados and kiwi fruit. Apart from subtropical plantation farming, the economy of the north coast is based on a mixture of tourism, dairy and beef cattle, and timber cutting. A number of resort towns lie along the coast, including Coffs Harbour and Port Macquarie. South of Port Macquarie is the beautiful Hunter Valley which includes Newcastle; with a population of over 250,000, it is the second largest city in New South Wales. Although Newcastle is well-known for its steel and coal factories, it is located on the ocean, and the smoke and industry seem far away when gazing out to sea at Nobby's Head. Equally, to the west and beyond the steelworks and the industrial concentration of the city lies the Hunter Valley, an incredibly rich and fertile region (thanks to the alluvial soils washed down by the Hunter River over thousands of years). It is also the largest area of lowland plains on the entire New South Wales coast, as the Great Dividing Range which hugs the coast from Tweed Heads to the Victorian border is pushed back here and the plains stretch far inland. As 'the garden' of New South Wales, this region produces out of all proportion to its size, with its agriculture ranging from dairy herds of Friesians to beef and horse studs, from fodder crops and orchards to vineyards. The first vines were planted in 1832 in the Pokolbin area north and west of Cessnock. Since then the area has developed a reputation for producing some of Australia's finest wines. Although the Hunter Valley only accounts for about two per cent of Australia's wine, its vineyards are known and respected internationally.

The longest of all of New South Wales' coastal rivers is the Hawkesbury which flows in a huge arc around the Sydney Basin before entering the sea at Broken Bay, north of the city. South of Sydney is the Georges River which, in part, forms the northern boundary of the wild and beautiful Royal National Park. A popular destination for day-trippers, particularly for people living in southern Sydney, it boasts a string of superb, isolated beaches and, at its southern tip, spectacular ocean views.

Beyond the Royal National Park is Wollongong, the state's third largest city and one of the country's major steel and coal centres. Nestling under a dramatic escarpment, this flourishing city is a strange mixture of alluring beaches and skies sulphur-filled from the steelworks. With a fascinating history, particularly regarding coal-mining, Wollongong has much more to offer than just beaches – it has a sophisticated shopping area, ideal fishing spots and beautiful Botanic Gardens.

From Wollongong to the Victorian border, the New South Wales south coast is a necklace of small fishing harbours. Among the most attractive is Eden which, in the nineteenth century, was one of the mainland whaling centres. For more than 100 years, Twofold Bay (above) has been home to one of Australia's largest fishing fleets.

Another attraction is Wollongong's famous, albeit modest, harbour, once the centre of all activity in the Illawarra. The reason for its early importance is obvious – on a coast where there are few natural harbours (a constant problem for the coal mines to the north of the city) it was simply the best available. The first settlers were woodcutters and graziers who hauled their logs up Bulli Pass and herded cattle on the rich coastal pastures. By the early 1820s, the harbour was being used to ship goods to and from Sydney. The 'village' which developed around the harbour became known as Wollongong – meaning 'look here comes the monster' in the language of the local Aborigines.

Of equal interest are the vantage points along the escarpment, offering some of the most spectacular scenery to be found anywhere in Australia. The view from Sublime Point includes Wollongong city, Port Kembla and the steelworks. However, when the humidity level is high, during rainy periods or when low banks of clouds blow in from the sea and push against the escarpment, the view is reduced to a white mist.

From Wollongong to the border of Victoria the coastal strip consists mostly of dairy country. Although there was a time when the green paddocks of the region were dotted with the soft browns of Jerseys and Guernseys, black-and-white Friesians rule supreme today. Driving along a winding country road, it is quite common to get caught behind a herd of Friesians making their way towards the milking sheds.

Behind the coastal strip lies the escarpment, boasting magnificent waterfalls, dark, narrow valleys with remnants of rainforest and extensive wildlife. These valleys lie close to the coast but beyond Kiama they fall back, making way for the wide floodplain of the Shoalhaven and the extraordinary, white sand arcs of the beaches which edge Jervis Bay. On the far south coast lies a series of attractive villages where fishing, timber and dairy industries intermingle. Eden, situated on the shores of Twofold Bay, was once a centre for whaling; Narooma, Bermagui, Tathra and Ulladulla all have thriving fishing fleets and towns while Kameruka, Bodalla and Bega are famous for their excellent dairy products, particularly cheeses.

Behind New South Wales' narrow coastal plain lies the Great Dividing Range. At some points this low-lying mountain range is 50-60 kilometres wide, but at others it stretches for up to 160 kilometres. In the north, the tablelands have an average elevation of about 750 metres, with the exception of the New England Ranges which rise to more than 1,200 metres. In the south, the tablelands form part of the Snowy Mountains, the highest mountain range in Australia. Apart from the obvious appeal of the Snowy Mountains' ski slopes, there are the underground delights of the Jenolan, Wombeyan, Yarrangobilly and Abercrombie caves, the splendid views of the Blue Mountains and the bracing country mountain air of the New England Ranges and the Southern Tablelands.

Recently the Snowy Mountains have become Australia's ski capital, with ski resorts, chalets, numerous ski-lifts and artificial snow-making machines (just in case winter doesn't provide enough natural snow) drawing tens of thousands for skiing holidays in winter. Spring and summer are spent bushwalking, visiting the beautiful Yarrangobilly Caves, exploring the old gold diggings at Kiandra and marvelling at the grandeur of the scenery.

Smudged by the distinctive smoky blue rising from the eucalypts, the Blue Mountains managed to halt the exploration of inland New South Wales for more than 20 years. The early explorers thought that all they had to do was follow a river to its source, climb the valley and cross the mountains. Every time they followed a river upstream, they came not to an ever-steepening valley or gorge, but to a waterfall which fell hundreds of metres over a sheer, unclimbable cliff. It was only in 1813 that Gregory Blaxland, William Charles Wentworth and Lieutenant William Lawson succeeded in crossing the mountains during their search to find new grazing land. The mountains which had presented such a challenge became a national park drawing thousands of visitors, a hill station where the wealthy can escape from Sydney's summer humidity, and a small-scale orchard area for apples, pears and cherries. The economy of the tablelands is based primarily on wool and cattle. Although some timber is cut in the area, tourism is gaining in importance, and a number of the larger towns – notably Armidale, Bathurst and Goulburn – have become important educational centres. Nevertheless it remains the home of Australia's prime merino grazing flocks and cattle studs.

Beyond the tablelands lie the western slopes, a narrow belt of land falling away from the tablelands and still enjoying adequate rainfall. The slopes are generally divided into three separate areas from north to south: the northern slopes which include major centres like Tamworth, Gunnedah, Narrabri and Warialda; the central slopes with cities like Dubbo and Forbes; and the southern slopes located between the Snowy Mountains and the dry plains of the Riverina. With the rainfall being high and frequent enough to guarantee regular feed, the slopes are good sheep and cattle grazing country, but are also known for their cold climate orchards – cherries, apples and pears, for example, are grown around Batlow and Bathurst.

Yet farther inland are the western plains. From the air, the marginal agricultural land, characteristic of the western two-thirds of New South Wales, seems to begin an hour away from Sydney. Rising above the Sydney Basin, the deep incisions of the Blue Mountains can be seen only minutes later, then the undulating slopes around Bathurst which rapidly give way to the flat plains of the western region. Although there is nothing wrong with the soils of the western plains, the area experiences low rainfall and has unreliable rivers. Blocked from the east by the Great Dividing Range and dissipated from the south and west by vast deserts, the rains which could turn it into an agriculturally rich domain never arrive. The western plains are predominantly wool country; only the orchards clinging to the banks of the Murray and the major mineral deposits of Broken Hill vary the economy of the area.

The Riverina Plains of New South Wales are typical Australian sheep country. Large properties, known as 'stations', are home to some of the world's finest merino sheep. This farmer is rounding up sheep (above) near the romantically named Riverina township of Wagga Wagga.

New South Wales can justifiably claim to be the most diverse state in Australia. Its position midway up the eastern coast of the continent and jutting in a roughly rectangular shape into the deserts of Central Australia means that although it only covers 10.4 per cent of the total area, it experiences all climates and most forms of vegetation, from snow gums to tropical rainforests, and can sustain most types of agriculture.

Although it does not form part of New South Wales, the Australian Capital Territory is surrounded by the state. It is here that the thriving and rapidly expanding national capital, Canberra, is situated, home to the country's public servants and politicians. Canberra is an artificial city which grew as a compromise; a city created not because of a natural need or certain advantages but as a result of interstate rivalries between New South Wales and Victoria. Where common sense would have demanded that either Sydney or Melbourne become the national capital (thus integrating federal politics and national administration into the real world of an existing city), political sense said it should be roughly equidistant from these two cities.

In 1908, after much debate, it was decided that 2,330 square kilometres of sheep grazing land in New South Wales would become the site for the capital city. Three years later the Australian Capital Territory was handed over to the Commonwealth Government, and that very same year a competition was launched for the design of a city for 25,000 people. Won by the American Walter Burley Griffin, the design, based on a series of geometrically precise circles and axes, was similar to the street patterns of Washington and Paris.

Today Canberra is a city of great aesthetic beauty with broad roadways, superb parklands, and many graceful buildings. The views across Lake Burley Griffin are breathtaking; from the War Memorial you can look straight across to the elegant new Parliament House on Capital Hill; from the shores of the lake, the reflections of buildings such as the High Court and the National Library are exceptional.

14

Queensland is a state rich in contradictions. It is the state with the warmest, most perfect weather but it is also the state most prone to the wild winds and drenching rains of cyclones. It is the state where the Australian Labor Party was formed, but for more than 30 years it was ruled by successive Conservative administrations. This sense of contradiction even extends to the state capital, Brisbane, still a big country town. Shorts are commonplace in this city of high finance, local timber buildings lie cheek-by-jowl with modern concrete and steel office blocks, and the name of ex-Premier, Johannes Bjelke-Petersen, like a town mayor, appears on 49 plaques on buildings in Queen Street.

Queensland covers a total area of 1,727,200 square kilometres, making it the second largest state in Australia. Within its boundaries there is great diversity – the southwestern corner is a desert while parts of Cape York and north Queensland consist of impenetrable rainforest and swampy, mangrove wetlands. It is therefore hardly surprising that most of the state's three million people cling to the coast. Brisbane, the extended cities of Whitsunday and Gold Coast, the holiday area of the Sunshine Coast, and the major cities of Bundaberg, Rockhampton, Townsville and Cairns, are home to most of the state's residents.

Some 650 kilometres north of Brisbane is the Tropic of Cancer, dividing the state equally between the tropical and subtropical zones. Similarly the Great Dividing Range, which starts about 200 kilometres south of Cape York, runs in a series of low-lying ranges and tablelands all the way down the eastern coastline, forming a natural division between the coastal plain and the vast Artesian Basin of western Queensland.

A recent survey revealed that 60 per cent of all tourists visiting Australia nominated Queensland as their primary destination, the reason being that from the Gold Coast in the south to Cairns and the Daintree Forest in the north, the coastal strip is a daisy chain of exceptional holiday resorts. Much more than just beaches (in fact for much of the year the threat of sharks and box jellyfish ensures very little ocean swimming), these comfortable holiday haunts boast swimming pools, tennis courts, golf courses and luxury restaurants, and offer trips to the Great Barrier Reef or journeys of exploration into the dense rainforest of the hinterland.

From the reefs and coral cays to the dry scrub of the Cape, from the rainforest tumbling into the sea to the spectacular waterfalls crashing over the escarpment, from the sugar cane plantations of the coast to the dairy herds of the Atherton Tablelands, the Queensland coast is breathtakingly beautiful, the landscapes and human activities rich in their diversity.

The reefs and islands from Cooktown to Townsville – Magnetic, Dunk, Hinchinbrook, Fitzroy, Green, Lizard and dozens of others – evoke all the romantic splendour of the tropics. Many are uninhabited. Those which are not, have only a few tiny, low-key resorts and walking paths established by the National Parks and Wildlife authorities. Tourists come to the area to marvel at the wonders of the Great Barrier Reef and to laze on the tropical beaches.

Every day the attraction of the living coral in all its bewildering variety and the exotic tropical fish sees hundreds of boats heading out from the wharves of Cooktown, Port Douglas, Cairns, Cardwell and Townsville. It was on these reefs that Captain James Cook ran aground and was forced to drag his boat up for repairs in the estuary of the Endeavour River at the presentday site of Cooktown.

The towns on the coast were all built for one reason: to provide port access, at first for the mineral wealth dug out of the hinterland, later to export sugar from towns like Innisfail, Ingham and Mourilyan. The construction of the ports posed no great challenge – the real challenge was to find routes from the tablelands down the steep escarpment. Not only were the early trailblazers confronted with sheer cliffs, but they also had to deal with dense rainforests and local Aborigines who were unimpressed with the invasion of their territory.

The escarpment is noted for its waterfalls, of which there are more than 100 between Townsville and Cooktown. While some like the Barron Falls near Kuranda and the Wallaman Falls behind Ingham are spectacular, others like those at Millaa Millaa and Malanda are small and intimate. Well-marked tracks, characterised by huge trees, bird-song in the canopy and a variety of floral species, lead to most

With its modern $200 million development Hayman Island (below), which has been one of the longest established tourist destinations in the Whitsundays islands on the Great Barrier Reef, is now regarded as the premier luxury destination in the Whitsunday group. Hayman Island is the only Australian resort hotel to be included in the 'Leading Hotels of the World' organisation. It is a true five-star resort.

of the falls, and afford visitors the ideal way to experience the rainforests. The greatest crime of the whole area is undoubtedly the Cape Tribulation Road, representing environmental vandalism at its very worst. In the wet season it turns to a quagmire of mud, and during the dry periods it is a mixture of dust, deep ruts and potholes. Forming an ugly, dirt-red gash across the face of the rainforest, it bleeds mud into the ocean whenever it rains.

The central Queensland coast is an area of vast fields of sugar cane, extraordinary tropical beauty, superb tourist locations like the Whitsunday Islands and beaches where enjoying the warm tropical sun simply becomes a necessity. Virtually the whole area, particularly the fertile plains in the coastal hinterland, is covered with sugar cane. In many of the towns, most notably Home Hill and Mirani, growers are so eager to maximise their crops that the sugar cane reaches right up to domestic gardens! To the south, the sugar farms tend to give way to cattle country. Rockhampton makes everyone aware of its abiding commitment to the cattle industry with life-size statues of bullocks at both ends of town.

Beyond the shore lies one of the true wonders of Australia – the Great Barrier Reef. Not only can it be seen from the moon, but it also has the distinction of being the largest structure built by living creatures on Earth. Stretching from Cape York to Bundaberg, the Reef is divided into four sections. The Far North extends from Cape York to Lizard Island; the Cairns section runs from Lizard Island to Dunk Island; the Central section from Tully to Mackay, including the Whitsundays; and the Capricorn section from Mackay to Bundaberg. It covers a total area of around 215,000 square kilometres and stretches along the coast for approximately 2,000 kilometres. Although it is thought that the reefs developed 25 million years ago when sea levels rose, its main development probably occurred as recently as 1.8 million years ago, with the modern coral reef only 8,000 years old.

The reef itself requires a peculiar combination of forces to grow. The minute stony corals which produce reefs develop best in sea water which doesn't drop below 22 °C or rise above 28 °C. They need a great amount of sunlight, should grow in relatively shallow water (below 60 metres there is not enough light) and survive and prosper where there is little muddying of the water by rivers or human pollution.

It is the central section, particularly the area around the Whitsundays, which is famous for its luxurious tourist resorts. These verdant islands were the ideal sites for hotels, marinas and, in the case of Hamilton Island, an airport for wide-bodied jet aircraft. In the Whitsunday area the continental shelf is no more than 9-16 metres deep, producing ideal circumstances for the coral to develop. The area to the south is much wider, stretching up to 200 kilometres out to sea, but the depths are greater. To the north the continental shelf extends only 30 kilometres out to sea and consequently the development of coral has occurred in a relatively narrow strip beside the coastline.

To the south of the Great Barrier Reef is the region known as the Sugar Coast, famous for its coastal attractions and resorts, including Fraser Island and towns like Bundaberg, Hervey Bay, Maryborough, Maroochydore and Caloundra. The European history of this area started in 1770 when Captain James Cook sailed up the coast, naming various features (most notably the Glasshouse Mountains). He saw Aborigines on the shore but made no attempt to explore the hinterland. The character of the area changed dramatically when, in 1842, Queensland (then still part of New South Wales) was opened to free settlers. Pastoralists moved large flocks of sheep into the area to take advantage of the good soils. The graziers, with their substantial production of wool, hides and tallow, forced the opening of a number of ports on the coast. Suddenly the whole area was booming.

In recent times the region has developed into one of the premier tourist attractions in Australia. The beaches are lovely, the accommodation extensive, the range of activities for visitors wide. Places like Hervey Bay, Noosa and Caloundra have become popular destinations for those fleeing the cold southern winters and wishing to have a holiday in the sun.

This development does not come close to that of the Gold Coast, visited each year by more than four million people. Running from Coolangatta to Tweed Heads, the 42-kilometre coastal strip sports golden beaches with ideal areas for

The Great Barrier Reef off the coast of north Queensland and near the city of Cairns, is a wonderland of reefs, coral cays and sand islands (above). Flying over the northern section of the reef, it is easy to appreciate the unspoilt beauty as well as the dangers which confronted the sailors who attempted to navigate through these shallow, treacherous waters.

sunbathing, body- and board-surfing, and an endless ribbon of holiday flats, motels, hotels, restaurants, fast food shops and chemists selling protection against the sun. Its drawcards are known all over Australia – Surfers Paradise, the Currumbin Bird Sanctuary, Palm Beach, Burleigh Heads, Jupiters Casino at Broadbeach, Seaworld at Southport, Dreamworld at Coomera. But the coastal experience is only half of the story of the Gold Coast. The mountains of the Great Dividing Range rising behind the coastal strip offer a unique perspective on the coastal development and the rich, undulating countryside falling away to the west.

Beyond the coast, Queensland is sparsely populated. The agricultural wealth of the Great Dividing Range and the slopes to the west of the range rapidly gives way to marginal land where the only centres of any size are either agricultural service centres or mining towns. Constantly battling to lure people away from the beautiful beaches of the Central Coast, The Central Highlands Tourist Organisation lists these unusual attractions: '... we have the largest sapphire-producing field in the world where some of the largest sapphires ever found have been mined (Anakie, Sapphire and Rubyvale); we have some of the biggest and most advanced machinery associated with coal-mining (Blackwater, Tieri, Blair Athol and Moura); one of Australia's finest collections of Aboriginal art (the Carnarvon Gorge); we have the largest sunflower-growing area in Australia (around Springsure); the largest seam of steaming coal in the world at Blair Athol; the largest citrus orchard in Australia in the Emerald irrigation area; the largest cotton-growing production in Queensland and the largest grain-growing property in Australia at 'Gordon Downs'.'

This is a region where two of the most fascinating episodes in Queensland's violent and lawless frontier history took place. It was during the 1850s that the area near Taroom gained its reputation as one of the bloodiest killing fields in the whole of Australia. The local Aborigines, the Yeeman, tried to retain their land by opposing the encroachment of European graziers. They fought with such determination that they were eventually wiped out. In the process a man named Billy Fraser almost certainly killed more than 100 members of the tribe, making him the greatest mass murderer in Australian history.

Harry Redford's tale is one of daring, chicanery and the outback's admiration for a criminal bushman. Redford stole 1,000 head of cattle from the vast 1.75-million acre Bowen Downs station near Muttaburra and drove them down the Cooper Creek into South Australia. That the explorers Burke and Wills had died attempting a similar journey only nine years earlier, goes to show just how daring this plan was. When Redford was captured and returned to Roma to be tried for cattle duffing, the local jury, so impressed by his bushcraft, acquitted him. The judge, incensed by the innocent verdict noted 'I thank God, gentlemen, that the verdict is yours, not mine!'. For the next two years, the criminal jurisdiction of the District Court at Roma was withdrawn.

North of the plains lies The Gulf Country, a vast tract of flat land stretching west from the slopes of the Great Dividing Range to the Northern Territory border and south to Cloncurry, Mount Isa and McKinlay. Essentially it is the bed of a vast inland sea which existed in the area some 100 million years ago. The last section of Queensland to be settled, it consists of pastoral country which is semi-arid (apart from the area around the Gulf where monsoonal rains sometimes fall) and where the population is in decline due to mechanisation. In this flat, featureless area you can travel hundreds of kilometres without passing another vehicle or seeing any great changes in the landscape. In fact, the overpowering impressions left by the area are of distance, isolation and loneliness, as well as admiration for the early settlers who came to this inhospitable land and managed to make a living from it.

The Gulf Country survives on two water supplies. Below the area lie the hot waters of the Great Artesian Basin (it covers 1,760,000 square kilometres, mostly in western Queensland). While often smelly and hardly fit for human consumption, it has sustained many of the large sheep and cattle stations in the area. For the traveller used to the sweet waters of the coast, the sulphurous smell of this water can be one of the most memorable aspects of any journey through the outback! The other water supply is produced by the rivers – the Barcoo, Thomson, Diamantina and Cooper Creek – which receive their water from far northern Queensland and can, in the rare event of flooding, provide good waterholes in the area for two to three years.

What then is the reason to experience the heat, the dust, the monotony and the bad roads of western Queensland? As one of the locals in Birdsville explains: 'I think that people like it out here because of the vast distances and the loneliness. It gives them a sense of space and a landscape which you can't imagine if you've spent all your life near the coast.'

Victoria is smaller, more refined and more under control than the other states. Its beach culture rivals the other states, but somehow the picture of sunworshipping Victorians doesn't quite fit the state's image. Equally, Fosters and the Carlton & United Breweries produce beer which is enjoyed all over the country, but the image of an 'Aussie' propping up a bar doesn't readily belong to Victoria. In the same vein, Melbourne is a bustling modern city with a high-rise skyline similar to that of Brisbane, Sydney or Perth but is still regarded as a leisurely, nineteenth-century, almost European city of wood-panelled, exclusive clubs where deals are clinched over a cigar and port. Victoria even has desert areas in the north and northwest of the state but its slogan, 'The Garden State' is so powerful that the idea of spinifex, gibber deserts and sand dunes is inconceivable. All in all, its identity is so firmly established that it is set far apart from the rest of the country.

Victoria is the smallest of the mainland states and the second smallest state in Australia. Covering just 227,620 square kilometres, it constitutes only three per cent of mainland Australia, but houses over 25 per cent of the country's inhabitants, making it the most densely populated state. Despite its smallness, Victoria has enjoyed long periods of predominance over its northern neighbour, New South Wales. The goldrush of the 1850s gave Melbourne an unprecedented affluence which meant that by 1888, when Australia celebrated its centenary, Melbourne had a larger population than Sydney. When the federation of Australian states was declared on 1 January 1901, it was Melbourne which became the seat of government until the federal Parliament House was built in Canberra.

Although some people will disagree, the rivalry between Victoria and New South Wales still exists. As far back as 1883, the French author Léon Paul Blouet observed: 'There never has been any war between New South Wales and Victoria, but simply a mean jealousy, which shows itself in all kinds of reprisals.' Although this competitiveness should be passé, it was the subject of David Williamson's 1980s play, *Emerald City* and is still the subject of jibes.

Perhaps the dispute between the two states began before Victoria had become a separate colony. Settled in an attempt to prevent the French from establishing a colony on Australian soil, Victoria, or the Port Phillip District as it was known, remained part of the colony of New South Wales until 1851. In 1803 Lieutenant David Collins, with a small group of convicts and free settlers, established a camp on Port Phillip Bay near the modern-day site of Sorrento, but he found the location unsatisfactory and moved to Van Diemen's Land the next year. It wasn't until 1824, when Hume and Hovell reached Port Phillip Bay, that the negative attitude towards the area changed. They reported large stretches of good grazing land and in 1826 a convict settlement was established at Western Port, only to be abandoned two years later. The real settlement of Victoria occurred when John Batman, a rogue who had made his fortune in Tasmania, took the law into his own hands and signed a treaty with the local Aborigines, 'purchasing' 600,000 acres from them. Subsequently this area grew into the modern city of Melbourne.

This was the beginning of Victoria's first boom period. In the next 20 years, settlers moved to claim large tracts of the state's grazing lands. The identity of the colony, although still a part of New South Wales, was formed in the early 1840s when it resisted attempts to have a penal colony established at Port Phillip. Finally, on 1 July 1851, the colony of Victoria was officially proclaimed. At the time, most of the state had been populated, with 80,000 people inhabiting the land and six million sheep spreading from the Murray River to the south coast. The colony had achieved its independence just as it was about to become vastly wealthy. In 1851, gold deposits were discovered at Clunes, Anderson's Creek, Ballarat, Bendigo and Mount Alexander. The impact the goldrush had on the state was remarkable – rural labourers downed tools and headed for the goldfields; cities became deserted; transportation and tools were sold at exorbitant rates; and ships brought tens of thousands of prospectors to the state. In only three years, Victoria's population rose from 80,000 to 300,000.

In 1850 imports into Victoria amounted to £750,000, the goods ranging from foodstuffs to building materials, but by 1854 imports had reached the staggering figure of £18 million. If the imports went through the roof, they were nothing when compared to the wealth generated by the goldfields – a total of 708,738,000 grams of gold, worth over £100 million, came out of Victoria in the 1850s.

The gold towns, some of them preserved as they were in the 1850s, are among Victoria's most important tourist draw-cards. The opportunity to experience the vitality which defined the state in its first few decades is readily available in historic villages and modern recreations. To appreciate the bustling, cosmopolitan nature of the goldfields, a visit to Sovereign Hill, a kind of gold-mining theme park near Ballarat, is an ideal introduction. Located on the site of the Sovereign Quartz Mining Company, the town has a 'diggings' where visitors can pan for gold and observe gold-mining techniques such as cradling and puddling. Ballarat also has a Gold Museum, a memorial to the Eureka Stockade and a Fine Art Gallery with an exceptional collection of Australian paintings. Bendigo is the other great historic gold-mining town. Its cosmopolitan goldrush days have left it with a varied range of attractions, including a Chinese joss house, a pottery founded by a Scottish entrepreneur in the 1850s, a number of wineries and the Central Deborah Mine, specially opened for tourists. Sandhurst Town, 12 kilometres out of Bendigo, is a local equivalent of Sovereign Hill.

To this day Victoria is rich in resources and has a strong economic base. Almost 36 per cent of the land is covered with forests, and some of the valuable timbers include eucalypts, mountain and alpine ash, as well as significant plantations of other softwoods and hardwoods. Primarily a fine wool and fat lamb producer, it has a sheep population which is only exceeded by those of New South Wales and Western Australia. The state is also a beef, wheat and dairy producer, and has a strong secondary industry base which developed as a result of the goldrush. The demand for rudimentary mining tools – winches, picks, shovels, and so on – and the continuing need for agricultural equipment meant that cities like Bendigo, Ballarat and Melbourne had all become substantial industrial centres by the 1860s.

The city of Melbourne lies at the heart of Victoria. With a population of 3.2 million, it sprawls around Port Phillip Bay and back into the hinterland. Like most Australian cities it has grown in keeping with its population, and Greater Melbourne now covers an area of well over 1,300 square kilometres. To the west and north it spreads over 20 kilometres from the central business district; to the east and southeast of the city it stretches 25 kilometres, with ribbons of urban development extending to the commuter belts of the Dandenong Ranges and the beachside suburbs around the eastern foreshores of the bay. Its average temperature is 15 °C; its annual rainfall 657 millimetres, rising to 889 millimetres in the ranges to the west of the city.

St Kilda beach (above) is one of the many popular summertime retreats for the residents of Melbourne. Located only a few kilometres from the city centre, the beach is well know for Brooks Jetty which juts out into Port Philip Bay.

Melbourne's economic origins lie in its pastoral potential. The first settlers grazed sheep, and bred horses and cattle on the plains and lower slopes of the surrounding hills. As the settlement grew, hay and potatoes became important crops and woodworkers moved into the nearby ranges, felling the best of the forest hardwoods. But it was gold that was the city's defining factor, bringing wealth, a denser population, roads and railway lines. Surrounding agricultural lands were developed in keeping with the growth of the population. Dairy farms provided the city with milk; crops of potatoes and domestic vegetables were grown on the plains while orchards of apples, pears, peaches, apricots and berry fruits were planted in the nearby mountains. Vines were grown in the river valleys, and gravels, stone and sand quarried.

Its central business district is a unique blend of heavy Victorian architecture characteristic of the city's boom period and modern high-rise buildings, and therefore maintains a colonial elegance within a dynamic, twentieth-century city. This is no accident. As long ago as 1971, committees were formed to plan Melbourne's development right up to the year 2000, partly to strike a balance between the city's modern development and its sense of history.

The rest of Victoria is equally diverse, offering the traveller enormous scope for exploration. Although it is the smallest mainland state, it has 1,200 kilometres of ocean coast, ranging from the dramatic cliffs of Cape Otway to the rock arches, rock stacks and blowholes around Port Campbell, and the seemingly endless Ninety Mile Beach. It has been argued by many that the Great Ocean Road, which starts at Torquay southwest of Melbourne and winds round the coast for 250 kilometres, reveals one of the most beautiful coastal areas in Australia. Particularly impressive along this road are the Twelve Apostles and the remnants of London Bridge to the west of Port Campbell. Originally constructed to create work for the unemployed during the Depression, the Great Ocean Road now enables millions of travellers to marvel at the endless vistas it provides.

In the centre of the state are the beautiful Grampian Ranges and the towns which shot up during the goldrush of the nineteenth century. To the west is the dry, near-desert of the Mallee; to the north the southern edges of the Snowy Mountains with their popular ski resorts. From the Snowy Mountains across to Swan Hill on the Murray River, the northeastern and north-central regions of Victoria encompass a great variety of climatic, geographic and economic areas. To the east, the area is mountainous and experiences significant snow falls and subzero temperatures in winter. Gradually the mountains, which lie at the edge of the Great Dividing Range, fall away to gently undulating slopes and by the time Swan Hill is reached, it is monotonously flat. Constituting most of the state's northern border with New South Wales, it is the Murray River which has done much to define the economy of the state. Once plied by steamers which carried produce to the Riverina sheep stations, it is now a popular retreat. A relaxing week can be spent cruising along the river, passing through the huge locks and visiting the old riverbank towns of Swan Hill, Mildura, Robinvale and Wentworth.

*L*ying to the south of Victoria and separated from the mainland by the dangerous Bass Strait is Tasmania, Australia's best-kept secret. This island, the smallest of all the Australian states, is so far removed from Europe and North America as to be almost dropping off the edge of the world. To feel this sense of isolation, one has only to stand on the cold, flat, windswept beaches on its west coast. The waves breaking on these beaches have rolled uninterrupted across the southern oceans from Argentina, passed below the Cape of Good Hope and have been whipped along by the icy winds of the Roaring Forties.

A sense of romance pervades Tasmania. There was a time when, for most mainland school children, Tasmania really didn't exist. They would sit in their classrooms, carefully tracing around the edges of a plastic map of Australia. The manufacturers of these maps, unable to devise a method of attaching Tasmania to the bottom of their mould, resolved the problem by leaving it off altogether!

But the main difference between Tasmania and the rest of Australia is the climate. Mainland Australians perceive themselves as living on the edges of a vast, dry desert on the one side and a necklace of beaches, lapped by blue waters and saturated by warm, subtropical sun on the other. It never even occurs to them that an entire state can live under dark rain clouds and be green and moist throughout. In fact, Tasmania defies all standard Australian images. This is not the land of the bronzed 'Aussie' or the great outdoors; instead, the winds blowing in from the Indian Ocean batter the island with their rains. All of this results in a sense of 'otherness', but it remains an area of great and undiscovered beauty. The island of Tasmania, King and Flinders islands and a number of smaller islands in Bass Strait which make up the outer limits of the state, cover an area of 67,800 square kilometres. The island state has a population of 470,300, of whom 183,600 live in the island capital of Hobart.

Named after Robert Hobart, Secretary of State for War and the Colonies at the time of its settlement, Hobart is located on the banks of the Derwent River. Given the wildness of Tasmania's weather, the state capital lies in quite a protected position. The mean annual rainfall is 630 millimetres, with the average monthly temperature being 21 °C in summer (February) and 11 °C in winter (July). Created specifically to keep the French out of Australia, Hobart was a thriving port with an estimated population of 5,000 by 1827. It was the centre of trade not only for Tasmania, but also for the sealers operating on the islands in Bass Strait and the whalers who were sailing the southern oceans.

In *Following the Equator* Mark Twain offered this eulogy to the city's charms: 'How beautiful is the whole region, for form, and grouping, and opulence, and freshness of foliage, and variety of colour, and grace and shapeliness of the hills, the capes, the promontories; and then, the splendour of the sunlight, the dim, rich distances, the charm of the water-glimpses! And it was in this paradise that the yellow-liveried convicts were landed, and the Corps-bandits quartered, and the wanton slaughter of the kangaroo-chasing black innocents consummated on that autumn day in May, in the brutish old time. It was all out of keeping with the place, a sort of bringing of heaven and hell together.'

Today Hobart is a place of exceptional beauty. Some of its highlights include the excellent Botanical Gardens which, for years, were tended by the bushranger Matthew Cash, and Battery Point with its mixture of history and modern charm, offering a unique opportunity to experience colonial Australia. But the central point to Hobart must be Constitution Dock and Salamanca Place. Each year festivities are the order of the day here when the boats taking part in the Sydney-Hobart race sail across the finishing line. Weekends see locals and visitors flocking to the outstanding Salamanca Markets, while Salamanca Place displays some of the finest examples of dockside Georgian warehouses (built between 1830-1850), now

In recent times tourism to Hobart has increased significantly by the establishment of Australia's first legal casino at Sandy Bay. The Wrest Point Hotel Casino (above), with its distinctive 64-metre-high cylindrical tower, now has several competitors on the mainland states. However, it still attracts significant numbers of tourists to its gambling tables.

converted into craft and gift shops, restaurants and galleries. Hobart's two great commercial drawcards are the Wrest Point Casino – located at Sandy Bay, it was the first legal casino in Australia – and the chocolate factory in Claremont. Each day the *Derwent Explorer* departs from Franklin Wharf and makes its way up river to the Cadbury factory. Apart from seeing how chocolate is produced, the visitor gets an opportunity to sample and purchase the product.

Around Hobart and in the valleys of the Derwent and Huon Rivers are the state's orchards. It is here that the bulk of the state's apples are grown, as well as apricots, lucrative crops of oil poppies and hops. Hop-growing is nearly as old as white settlement in Tasmania – as early as 1823, William Shoobridge planted hops in the Providence Valley and ever since then, the Shoobridge family has been associated with Tasmanian hop production. Recently the romantic image of hop-pickers has given way to a capital-intensive industry based on mechanical hop-pickers and drying machines.

To the north of Hobart, the island's main north-south road joins the state capital with Launceston. The drive between these two centres gives visitors an opportunity to experience what Australia must have been like in the nineteenth century. Villages like Ross and Richmond have been magnificently preserved and now form the focus of the tourist industry. The centre of the island is made up of a plateau, with a series of glacial lakes and a number of major mountains, most notably Mount Ossa, Ben Lomond, Cradle Mountain and Eldon Park. All of these mountains rise above 1,400 metres.

The northwest coastal strip, which runs from the port of Devonport to Stanley with its famous 'Nut' (a remarkable rocky outcrop), is recognised as the best land on the island. The soils are rich, the rainfall averages around 960 millimetres and the average temperatures are mild – ideal conditions to raise beef and dairy cattle, and grow potatoes and peas. The northern and northeastern section, stretching from Devonport across the estuary of the Tamar River to Scottsdale and around the coast to St. Helens and Scamander, is sparsely inhabited agricultural land which produces good crops of potatoes, wheat and barley. Located off the northern coast, King Island has become famous for its dairy products, and its butters, cheeses and creams (particularly clotted cream) are now recognised as the best dairy products produced in Australia.

Conserving the environment is a top priority in Tasmania. Because of its location and the inhospitable nature of its terrain, large areas have remained unpopulated. Indeed the southwestern corner of the island has no permanent settlement and has often been marked on maps with 'unexplored', a label of true desolation. Equally important is the preservation of the unique fauna and flora found in Tasmania. The Huon pine, for example, can grow for well over 2,000 years. The Tasmanian devil, once an inhabitant of mainland Australia, is now restricted to the island. And the Tasmanian tiger is, perhaps, still hiding in the state's wilderness. More than these reasons for the preservation of the environment, there is the enduring truth that Tasmania is an island of breathtaking natural beauty despoiled by humanity. Already the beauty of Lake Pedder, with its white sands and ring of jagged mountains, has been drowned by the Tasmanian Hydro-Electricity Authority.

One of the most remarkable examples of what humanity can do to the environment can be seen at Queenstown on the island's west coast. The hills look more like a moonscape than an area which once had rich, dense forests. The timber was originally felled to supply the local copper smelter, and the fumes from the smelter did the rest. Yet beyond this devastation lie undulating hills, often covered in morning mists.

Only 37 kilometres away is Strahan on the edge of Macquarie Harbour, the last outpost of civilisation on the west coast and surely one of the loneliest places on earth. Named after Governor Lachlan Macquarie, this 50-kilometre-long harbour opens to the sea through the narrow Hell's Gates and receives the waters of the King and Gordon rivers. Created by the British as the ultimate penal colony in 1821, it was closed down in 1833 when the convicts were removed to Port Arthur. They worked on a nearby coal seam and rowed across the harbour each day to cut down the stands of Huon pine which edged the waters. Despite its brief history as a convict settlement, the harbour remains virtually untouched, and on a clear day is like a near-perfect mirror. Its waters are stained by the brown button grass which grows on the river banks and its shores heavily wooded.

Environmentalists were triumphant when a dam proposed by the Tasmanian Hydro-Electricity Authority was stopped and the whole area, including the Aboriginal art in Fraser Cave and the white waters of the Franklin River, were preserved under a World Heritage order. As the Tasmanian-born writer, Peter Conrad, observed: 'Sometimes the island resembles a subsiding Atlantis. The Nut, the volcanic knob at Stanley on the northwest coast, is a mountain which has abruptly dived into the sea, leaving only a flattened, furrowed summit showing. Tasmania was separated from the mainland when the land-bridge over Bass Strait caved in; ever since the prehistoric calamity, the island has been working to complete the process by submerging itself. Its hydro-electric schemes answer a deep-down wish to drown the land.'

For bushwalkers and backpackers Tasmania has walking paths, mountain climbing and white-water rafting to challenge the hardiest and most committed. For mainlanders wishing to escape the dry, blistering heat of summer, it offers a cool retreat. For families it offers such a diversity of entertainment – from watching the Tasmanian devil at Cradle Mountain, through cruises across Macquarie Harbour, to exploring the island's convict past at Port Arthur – that everyone will find something to fascinate them. Recently Tasmania has also become a popular retreat for people wishing to practise an alternative lifestyle. The Huon Valley and the rural areas around Hobart have been settled by potters, woodworkers and craftspeople who sell their wares in the gift shops which have sprung up in the city centre.

*H*istory has been kind to South Australia. The two events – convict transportation and the goldrush – which did so much to define the character of most of Australia, are missing from this part of the country's early history. The colony was a careful exercise in planning. In 1829 Edward Gibbon Wakefield proposed a scheme for systematic colonisation. The idea of selling big areas of Crown Land and using the money to pay for the emigration of labourers became a reality in 1834 when the South Australian Association was formed. Human optimism being what it is, a fleet of eight ships captained by John Hindmarsh left England and arrived at Holdfast Bay on 28 December 1836.

Although the land near the site of modern-day Adelaide had been surveyed and sold by March 1837, surveys of country areas were delayed. Property speculation became the colony's main industry. By 1840, only three years after the first settlement, the colony had a population of 14,000 free settlers but was totally bankrupt. Some 150 years later, South Australia is known as the centre of the Australian wine industry, has gained a reputation for its efficient secondary industry, has a strong mining base (particularly on the Eyre Peninsula) and boasts a diversity of landscape and climate which turns it into a state of great charm and beauty.

When Australians think of South Australia, images come to mind which are unique to the state – Adelaide, its beautiful parks and churches and the slow-flowing River Torrens. Then there are the images of the painter Hans Heysen's beloved Hahndorf and the Flinders Ranges. Born in Munich, Germany in 1877, Heysen was a prolific artist and his water-colours of the Australian bush, with their subtle lighting and massive, strongly drawn gum-trees, became symbols of the Australian landscape. Another image of South Australia is that of its vineyards and wines – it was in the valleys of this state that the Australian wine industry established its reputation for quality. Today the Barossa Valley, Clare Valley and towns like Reynella, McLaren Vale, Penola, Seppeltsfield and Coonawarra are recognised internationally as the homes of some of the world's finest wines.

For all its apparent gentility and sophistication, South Australia is fundamentally similar to the other mainland states. The bulk of the state's population clings to the coast and the immediate environs of the state capital. As the land sweeps north from the Spencer Gulf and the Murray Valley, it becomes more and more marginal so that most of the north of the state is dry, unusable desert incapable of sustaining any kind of life.

South Australia is Australia's third largest state. It covers a total of 984,400 square kilometres of which just under half is nothing more than deserts of saltbush, endless sand dunes and flat, waterless lakes. Only about one-third of the state – the area of the Flinders and Mount Lofty Ranges, the Eyre, Yorke and Fleurieu peninsulas, the Coorong and the Murray River Valley – is deemed to be economically viable. Most of this area experiences a Mediterranean climate with a cold, moist winter and a dry, hot summer. These conditions exist on the coast but weaken further inland, eventually degenerating into areas where the annual rainfall is below 125 millimetres and summer temperatures soar into the 40s.

South Australia's economic base includes the rich deposits of uranium at Roxby Downs, open-cut coal deposits in the Leigh Creek area, natural gas in the Cooper Basin, vast iron-ore deposits at Iron Knob, Iron Monarch and Iron Baron, copper at Burra and Kanmantoo, and opal-mining at Coober Pedy, Andamooka and Mintabie. The state is also reliant on agriculture, ranging from vines, olives, figs and oranges to wheat, barley, oats and sheep-farming. Orange juice from the Murray River area and wines from the Barossa Valley can be found throughout the country.

With a low and unreliable water supply, South Australia has developed a sophisticated system of water storage and conservation. The Snowy Mountains Hydro-Electricity Scheme feeds melting snow into the system, ensuring adequate water during the long, dry summer months. In recent times the resources of the Murray River have also become a vital part of the state's economic well-being.

Adelaide is a city quite unlike any other in Australia, its country town friendliness interweaved with an urbanity which gives it a distinctively European feel. It is a city which can still be traversed, from north to south through the 'main street', King William Road, without having to contend with traffic jams. With a population of slightly over a million people, Adelaide is the Australia's fourth largest city. It is one of the country's few planned cities and its broad streets, all neatly laid out in a grid pattern, have a sense of openness and cleanliness. With an average rainfall of 560 millimetres and a temperature range from 12 °C in July to 23 °C in February, its design lends itself perfectly to outdoor living, its malls and parks encouraging leisurely walks and picnics.

In the last 50 years, Adelaide has, like all Australian cities, turned into a sprawling city with suburbs spreading nearly 40 kilometres to the south, reaching almost to the McLaren Vale wine-growing area. To the east they nestle into the Adelaide Hills and, to the north, they spill into the industrial town of Elizabeth.

Adelaide is known for its attention to the arts: its Festival Centre on the banks of the River Torrens boasts three theatres and an outdoor amphitheatre, and the Adelaide Festival of Arts has attracted well-known artists from all over the world. And Adelaide, for its population, has more restaurants than any other Australian city. The city's attractiveness was aptly captured by the little-known novelist, Doris Egerton Jones: 'Adelaide is just a beautiful place; we drove through its nice broad streets and past the Parklands. I think the big stretches of green bordered with trees look so cool and countrified within three minutes of the heart of the city. And then the little gardens of scarlet and purple dotted amongst the close-kept lawns and the bank of colour on the Torrens side, and the low riot of gold and green in the shade of the plane-trees before the Oval.'

For visitors travelling from the eastern states, their first view of the beautiful Flinders Ranges in South Australia is from Hancocks Lookout (above). For most of the year the ranges are dry, near desert but after the winter rains they come alive with wildflowers and the grasses which briefly cover the hills with verdant pastures.

Beyond the city are the famous Adelaide Hills, now one of South Australia's most popular holiday destinations. The small villages which nestle into the hills — Birdwood, Cudlee Creek, Blackwood, Clarendon, Glen Osmond, Gumeracha, Hahndorf, Lobethal and Mount Barker — are a mixture of tourist attractions (museums and gift shops) and rural housing for people eager to escape from Adelaide's city life.

The centrepiece of the whole area is Hahndorf — the oldest surviving German settlement in Australia. First inhabited by German émigrés in 1840, Hahndorf is a little piece of Germany on Australian soil. At present the town is a popular tourist haunt offering galleries, crafts by local craftspeople, Teutonic bakeries and restaurants specialising in German cuisine.

The Mediterranean climate of South Australia convinced the early settlers that this was an ideal area for vineyards, and as early as 1837, less than a year after the arrival of the state's first settlers, John Barton Hack had planted grape vines in North Adelaide. But the most famous wine area is the Barossa Valley where wine has been made commercially since the 1840s. The valley is only 30 kilometres long and eight kilometres wide but the soil, temperatures and rainfall are all ideal for wine-making. Over 100 kilometres north of the Barossa Valley, and surrounded by the Mount Lofty Ranges, is the Clare Valley. Vineyards were introduced into this area in 1848 by the Austrian Jesuit priest, Father Aloysius Kranewitter. Today more than half of all grapes grown in Australia are harvested in South Australia, which boast over 150 wineries. One of the great claims of the South Australian wine industry is that it produces all kinds of wines from reds to whites, champagnes, after-dinner Sauternes, ports and sherries, ranging from award-winning wines to mass-produced flagon and cask wines.

North of the Clare Valley, the Flinders Ranges, the most extensive mountain range in the state, stretch 500 kilometres from Crystal Brook to the southern edges of the Lake Eyre Basin. About 650 million years ago the range formed part of the sea bed. Its subsequent uplift has resulted in a series of fossils of sea creatures — trilobites and worms, recognised as the oldest fauna fossils on earth — appearing in the rock formations in the range. The beauty of the ranges, particularly in spring with its clear blue days and fields of native flowers, has resulted in a dramatic increase in tourism. Wilpena Pound is an exquisite area which has become popular with walkers and explorers.

At the entrance of Gulf St. Vincent is Kangaroo Island, the third largest island off the Australian coast. The absence of predators and any large human settlement has resulted in wildlife unthreatened by humans, allowing visitors to walk among the seals at Seal Bay. To the east of Kangaroo Island are the vast sand dunes (they stretch for over 145 kilometres) known as the Coorong, one of South Australia's premier national parks. The poet Will Ogilvie wrote of the area: 'It is sunset in the Coorong, the ribbon of blue water that divides the ninety mile desert from the sea on the coast of South Australia below Adelaide. Behind the low sandhills the sun is going down in a regal crimson splendour; the water takes a peculiar greenish purple tint beside us, fading away into crimson and gold between the brown of the sand hummocks and the dark green of the mallee scrub on the desert side.'

On the western shore of Gulf St. Vincent lies a long, narrow promontory known as the Yorke Peninsula. The poorness of the vegetation and the lack of permanent water inhibited settlement and it wasn't until the 1860s, when copper was discovered at Wallaroo and Moonta on the western coast of the peninsula, that any permanent townships were established. For the next 60 years the area boomed. As the copper mining declined, the wet winters and dry summers offered ideal growing conditions for wheat and barley, and today the peninsula is the centre of South Australia's barley production.

The Eyre Peninsula, the western coastline of South Australia, was the first part of the state to be sighted by Europeans. In 1627 the Dutch explorer Peter Nuyts sailed across the Great Australian Bight, sighted the peninsula but, deciding not to land, turned back and headed north towards Batavia. At best the Eyre Peninsula is marginal land. It rarely rises above 150 metres, and the soils are characteristically poor and sandy. The rainfall across most of the area averages little more than 250 millimetres per annum. In consequence the main agricultural activities of the area are sheep-grazing and wheat-farming, one of the distinctive features of the peninsula being the clusters of wheat silos dotted throughout the countryside. The wheat harvest is duly transported to the excellent port facilities at Port Lincoln where it is shipped overseas.

Port Lincoln is also the home of a highly successful fish cannery. The waters of both Spencer Gulf and the southern ocean yield a rich harvest of blue-fin and striped tuna, whiting, shark, garfish, snapper, salmon and, in the field of seafood delicacies, southern rock lobsters, western king prawns, abalone, scallops and Coffin Bay oysters.

To the north and west of the Eyre Peninsula is desert. In the 1950s this barrenness was seen as ideal for a rocket launching station and nuclear experiments. Woomera was established as a township in 1948 by the Australian government, with the aim to turn it into a base for service and scientific personnel working at the Weapons Research Establishment. By 1964 it had become a working missile station. In 1966 rockets which were part of the European ELDO space program were launched from Woomera and the following year the first Australian satellite was launched.

In 1955 the nearby centre of Maralinga, in the inhospitable western desert, was established as a base for British nuclear testing. The area was deemed to be both uninhabited and uninhabitable, but subsequent evidence has shown that Aborigines were living in the desert at the time of the experiments and if they weren't killed, they certainly would have suffered serious health problems as a result of the radioactive fallout.

The western strip of coastal South Australia is the southern limit of the Nullarbor Plain, an arid, scrubby, flat limestone plateau which has been chewed away for millions of years by the relentless seas of the southern ocean. On the coast the plain falls away dramatically in a series of sheer cliffs. The Nullarbor plain experiences less that 250 millimetres of rainfall per annum but because of the porous nature of the limestone this rain drains underground so quickly that streams cannot form. Recently elaborate cave systems have been found under the plain's harsh exterior. The Mullamullang cave in the Madura district is now recognised as the largest cave in Australia. Equally the Koonalda cave has evidence of Aboriginal habitation dating back 18,000 years. Evidence of cave paintings and flint quarrying in the region has also been found.

*T*he most enduring images left on travellers passing through the Northern Territory are the flatness of the terrain and the vast, underpopulated isolation of the whole region. It is quite possible for tourists to drive for 200-300 kilometres without passing a single service station or seeing another human being. Given the inhospitable nature of the terrain, it is therefore hardly surprising that the territory boasts a population of only 168,600 spread over 1,346,200 square kilometres.

The history of white settlement in the territory is one of a constant struggle against adversity. In 1861-62 John McDouall Stuart, after two previously unsuccessful attempts, finally crossed the country from south to north. The subsequent route for the Overland Telegraph Line was worked out by using Stuart's maps and journals. In turn the repeater stations which were established at Port Darwin, Yam Creek (Pine Creek), Daly Waters, Powells Creek, Tennant Creek, Barrow Creek, Alice Springs and Charlotte Waters along the Overland Telegraph route became the first communities in the Territory. The pastoralists compounded this by using the Telegraph Line as a stock route. To improve the water supply along the track, bores were sunk and often a small community developed around these bores.

The Northern Territory was once described by Sumner Locke Elliott as '... this lonely strip of barren and seemingly endless sandy waste of ant-hills and stunted trees – thick, hot red sand in the winter time and a sea of mud during the dreaded "Wet".' This is certainly an apt, if harsh, description of much of the Barkly Tablelands, Top End and Katherine region. People who arrive expecting tropical rainforest in the north and sandy desert landscapes in the south will be disappointed. Darwin and the 'Top End' are the true tropics of the Northern Territory. The climate of warm days in winter, hot and oppressive days in October, and the long, hot 'wet' from late October to March, is classically monsoonal and the vegetation typical tropical savanna woodland. The area's prosperity has historically relied on Darwin's importance as a port (both for transportation and for fishing and pearling), the cattle industry, and the mineral wealth of the area which over the years has changed from gold to uranium. Today it is increasingly geared to tourism, which ranges from exploring places of natural beauty like Kakadu National Park and Litchfield Park to visiting 'crocodile parks' and other tourist attractions.

The Top End seems to be obsessed with reptiles. On the Stuart Highway south of Darwin people can watch vast numbers of crocodiles being fed at Crocodile World; on the road to Kakadu, hundreds of species of snake and lizard can be viewed at Reptile World; and then there are the trips down the muddy estuarine waters of the Alligator and Adelaide Rivers to see saltwater crocs basking in the mud.

The natural highlights of the Top End include the waterfalls which tumble across the escarpments (particularly Wangi Falls, the Florence Falls in Litchfield Park and the beautiful Jim Jim Falls in Kakadu), the fascinating magnetic anthills, the billabongs and wetlands with their myriad bird life, and the dramatically beautiful tropical sunsets and thunderstorms.

Positioned far enough south to avoid the worst excesses of 'the wet' and far enough north to avoid the harshness of The Centre's desert continentality, the Katherine area is buoyed up by extensive beef cattle holdings, the mineral wealth which exists from Pine Creek north to Kakadu National Park, and a burgeoning tourist industry. In the winter the temperature in the area sits on a daily high of around 20 °C and the rainfall figure is low. In summer the combination of an average temperature of 34 °C and monthly rainfall ranging between 150-200 millimetres (the annual rainfall is about 900 millimetres) produces a bearable tropical humidity.

The region stretches from the drier areas of Victoria Downs and Timber Creek across to the mangrove swamps of the Gulf Coast near Roper Bar. This area is basically flat, with the obvious exception of the gorges in the Katherine region and the hilly country around Pine Creek. With the beauty of the Katherine Gorge (one of the wonders of the Territory, indeed, one of the wonders of Australia), the large number of excellent swimming holes, the limestone formations which have produced Cutta Cutta Caves, the hot springs at Mataranka and the rich variety of fauna and flora (including the ubiquitous ant hills), the area offers visitors a wide range of delights.

The Barkly Tablelands, an area of some 130,000 square kilometres spreading from north-western Queensland into the Northern Territory, were first explored by Ludwig Leichhardt in 1845 and opened up by the famous stockman, Nat Buchanan, who travelled from Rocklands Station in Queensland across the tablelands to the Overland Telegraph Line in 1877. In the 1890s the area became legendary as the great herds of beef cattle were driven across the semi-desert areas from the fertile Kimberley into north Queensland. During the war, with the aid of US funds, the Barkly Highway was built from just north of Tennant Creek across to Cloncurry via Mount Isa. It was subsequently upgraded so that today it is the main artery for all transportation through the area.

Alice Springs is the one place in the Northern Territory where a traveller could easily spend two or three weeks. The diversity of activities and sights, and the possibility of seeing all of the key elements of the Territory's history and 'personality' in one area, make The Alice a kind of microcosm of the appeal of the whole of the Northern Territory.

The MacDonnell Ranges sprawl out to the east and the west of The Alice, starkly denuded as though the flesh of 1,000 million years has been stripped away and all that is left are the bare bones, the essence of the earth, rising up in jagged, blood-red cliffs which stand out against the cobalt blue

North of Uluru lie the 36 smaller monoliths known as Kata Tjuta (The Olgas). The highest is Mount Olga which rises to 546 metres. The Olgas (below) are spread across an area of some 3,500 hectares and the distance around the group is about 22 kilometres. It is thought that Kata Tjuta may have once been one gigantic monolith many times the size of Uluru.

of the desert skies and the white ghost gums which abound in the region. Then there are the gorges with their relic vegetation, pools of water and the flora and fauna, ranging from snakes and lizards to the black-footed rock wallabies and dingoes which can be seen padding their way through the bush or scrounging for food in the car park at Standley Chasm. There are endless opportunities to go bushwalking through Ormiston Gorge and Pound, around the rim of Kings Canyon, up the valley at N'Dhala Gorge, or to the mine sites at Arltunga. And, most importantly, there are Uluru (formerly Ayers Rock) and Kata Tjuta (formerly the Olgas), rising out of the flat wastelands of the desert to mesmerise travellers with their changing colours and strange, haunting spirituality.

The first sight of Uluru is something that visitors never forget. It sits in the centre of Australia, nearly 1,500 kilometres south of Darwin and 500 kilometres from Alice Springs. It is surrounded by desert and rises 348 metres above the surrounding countryside. The rock is now owned by the local Aborigines who, in 1985, were given the title to the rock and who, in turn, granted the Australian National Parks and Wildlife Service a 99-year lease on the park. To the north of Uluru lie the 36 smaller monoliths known as Kata Tjuta. The highest of the monoliths is Mount Olga which rises to 546 metres.

*D*uring the past decade Western Australia has undergone some remarkable changes. For years the popular image of Western Australia, particularly in the eastern states, was of a vast, sparsely populated state which, somehow, wasn't really part of Australia proper.

Western Australia is rich in history. It is the state where, in the seventeenth and eighteenth centuries, many Dutch sailors frequented the coastline. Every Australian child knew the story of Dirck Hartog who, on 25 October 1616, nailed a pewter plate to a post at Cape Inscription. That strange, lonely tale caught everyone's imagination. The idea that the plate gazed forlornly out across the Indian Ocean for 80 years before Willem de Vlamingh took it down, added to the images of barrenness and isolation.

Then there was Broome – the most exotic of places where the pearl fishers lived; where luggers sailed out to sea and men were lowered to the ocean floor in equipment which made them look like creatures from outer space. The stories told of pearl fishers who had died of decompression sickness (the 'bends'), of the Japanese cemetery (the largest in Australia), and of the storms which blew up out of nowhere and decimated the pearling fleet, all helped to create an image of a mystifying outpost a world away from civilisation. There was also the story of the Durack family who carved a cattle empire out of the wild, fertile lands of the Kimberley and of little Paddy Hannan, the compulsive gold fossicker, who literally tripped over a nugget and found Kalgoorlie, which was to become one of the greatest gold-mining towns in the world.

Beyond that the history of the state was a mystery. No one ever recounted the remarkable story of the *Catalpa*, the US whaling ship which stole six Irish Fenians from Bunbury in 1875 and smuggled them to freedom in the USA. Or of Major Peter Egerton Warburton who made the perilous journey from Alice Springs to the Western Australian coast or A.C. and F.T. Gregory who, in the 1840s and 1850s, carried out extensive explorations along the continent's western coastline and hinterland.

Covering a vast 2,525,500 square kilometres with 7,000 kilometres of coastline, Western Australia is the largest state in the country. It is an extensive, low-lying plateau which rarely rises above 600 metres. The only variations are the narrow coastal plain which runs down the west coast from Broome to Albany, the low-lying Stirling Ranges in the south and the Hamersley Range in the northwest.

The state's climate ranges from the monsoonal wet season which sweeps across Wyndham, the Kimberley and the Broome area between December and March, to the arid desert in the west and the mild Mediterranean climate of cool, wet winters and warm, dry summers in the south. The extremes of the state are symbolised by the town of Marble Bar which is widely recognised as Australia's hottest place. From 31 October 1923 to 17 April 1924 a temperature of 100 °F (38 °C) was recorded every day – the longest heat wave ever recorded in Australia.

Beyond the coastal plain the state is an endless, uninhabited desert. Less than 15 per cent of its population lives in rural areas and over 90 per cent lives in the fertile South-West Land Division which encompasses both Perth and Fremantle.

At points along the vast Nullarbor Plain travellers are warned that, although the land is flat and there is hardly a tree in sight, there is a constant danger from wandering camels, wombats and kangaroos. The aim may be to save the animals, but they could cause considerable damage to a vehicle and help is usually hundreds of kilometres away.

Named after the Scottish birthplace of the British Secretary of State, George Murray, Perth is located on the banks of the Swan River. The site was originally chosen by Captain James Stirling as a suitable location for a colony. Initially the British government rejected the proposal but when Stirling returned to England in 1828, he succeeded in generating enthusiasm for the idea and the first colonists arrived a year later. The colony was the first in Australia to be developed entirely by free settlers. It wasn't until 1850 that convicts arrived and by that time the basic structure of the settlement had already been established.

Perth is a charming, attractive city – its elegant riverside parks, the network of freeways and the languid beauty of the Swan River all combine to give it grace and distinction. Its economic function within the state has changed since its inception. In 1832 it had a smaller population than Fremantle, but enjoyed a minor boom in the 1830s and 1840s when the area around it started producing substantial amounts of wool and wheat. Another boom occurred in the 1890s with the goldrush at Coolgardie and Kalgoorlie. In the 1950s a number of industrial suburbs grew up on the outskirts of the city and in the 1960s and 1970s a property boom occurred as an indirect result of the iron and nickel booms of the time.

In his novel *City of Men* Gavin Casey astutely observes: 'When the crop fails the city fails. Townies who ask how the wheat-belt is looking aren't just making conversation. They want to know. It's a wheat-growing city, if you can understand the term. It doesn't make anything. It just buys and sells things, and the only places to which it can sell anything except the wheat and wool and gold are the goldfields, the wheat-belt and the grazing areas.'

This state's South-West region is one of the most beautiful and interesting areas in Australia. Here are coastlines of breathtaking beauty, with sand dunes pushing up against the wildflowers which abound on the headlands. Here are cliff faces, headlands, promontories and capes all carved out of rugged granite by the wind and rain and the pounding forces of the Southern and Indian Oceans. Here is an area where waves of 10-15 metres can suddenly appear on a calm day, grim reminders of wild storms which may have occurred days before in the Southern Ocean, and wash unsuspecting fishermen into the sea (the first European 'settlers' in the area were in fact the whalers and sealers who sought protection from the storms of the Southern Ocean). And behind these coastal wonders lie the huge karri and jarrah hardwood trees which have made this one of the most important timber areas in the country. Small timber towns nestle in valleys with the blue smoke from the sawmill wisping up against the monotonous grey-green of the surrounding vegetation. Seemingly offering everything – the towns in the forests are quiet and attractive, the coastal resorts underdeveloped, the scenery spectacular – the area has boomed as a tourist destination in recent times.

The Southern Coastal region of Western Australia, sometimes known simply as the southeast, includes the magnificent Stirling Ranges and Porongurups, as well as some of the most dramatic and awe-inspiring coastline in the country. It is an area of extensive national parks, of white sand beaches and aquamarine seas, of rugged and unusual cliff formations, and old townships like Albany and Esperance.

In the 1890s thousands of prospectors poured into Western Australia through Albany and Esperance, making their way north and west to the goldfields of the Coolgardie-Kalgoorlie region. However, the area did not prosper for most of the twentieth century. The rainfall was reliable but much of the coastal soil was poor and lacking in nutrients and it wasn't until the 1950s that scientists found that trace elements could enrich the soil. In the case of Esperance, for example, the amount of useful agricultural land in the area increased from 8,000 to 400,000 hectares in 30 years as a result.

Further east, the Eucla region is notable for the longest distance between towns anywhere in Australia. From Norseman in Western Australia to Penong in South Australia is 1,131 kilometres and all that lies between these two settlements is a series of roadhouses providing the traveller with food, accommodation, fuel and garage repair facilities. This area encompasses parts of the Nullarbor Plain, but the Nullarbor (that is, desert with no trees) lies across the border in South Australia, as do the dramatic cliffs of the Great Australian Bight, the one truly awe-inspiring experience one has when travelling across the Nullarbor. All that is left in this sparse and barren region of Western Australia are nearly 700 kilometres of road, vast deserts, some fascinating caves, many low-lying sand dunes pushed up against the continent by the harsh winds that seem to blow off the Southern Ocean all day long, and the fascinating old Eucla Telegraph Station standing, half hidden by sand dunes, a few kilometres from Eucla. To the north and west of Eucla is the Goldfields region which covers the semi-desert area lying to the east of the wheatbelt. It is an area of gently undulating country with salt lakes, granite outcrops and hardy semi-arid flora.

In the decade 1890-1900, miners, fossickers and prospectors poured into the area around Kalgoorlie and Coolgardie. The population of Western Australia leapt from a mere 29,000 to 110,000 and most of that increase was directly attributable to gold. The growth of the area was also the result of the work of the engineer C.Y. O'Connor whose vital water pipeline was completed and opened in 1902. The unreliable and sparse water supply of both Coolgardie and Kalgoorlie was replaced by a reliable supply which came from Mundaring, hundreds of kilometres to the east. Unlike most desert areas, where brilliant skies and harsh landscapes are the main attractions, the fascination of the Goldfields is in its towns. Trips to Coolgardie and Kalgoorlie are essential and visits to their modern equivalents, Norseman and Kambalda, informative.

The coast north of Perth includes the most dramatically beautiful displays of wildflowers to be seen anywhere on the Australian mainland, the spectacular cliffs of Kalbarri, the strange, sentinel-like Pinnacles in the Nambung National Park, a cluster of lazy little fishing villages and the Abrolhos Islands. Further north is the Gascoyne, a region of remarkable diversity, with attractions including the beautiful Ningaloo Coral Reef, peculiar domed stromatolites, the shell beach at Shark Bay, dolphins at Monkey Mia, game-fishing off the coastal islands, thousands of kilometres of unspoiled sand beaches, the largest monolith in Australia (much larger than Uluru), the extraordinary, old gold-mining towns of Cue and Meekatharra, Aboriginal art in the hinterland around Cue and Mount Magnet, a river that flows upside down, and the place where the first words from the moon reached Earth.

The Gascoyne is a sparsely populated area where the rainfall is so low that most activity is marginal. In Mount Magnet, for example, the average rainfall is only 228 millimetres per annum and even on the coast a tourist town like Denham has to rely on a desalination plant to provide fresh water for the tens of thousands of visitors who come to the region each year.

The Pilbara is an area of mines, mining towns and port facilities. In the last 30 years the four major mining companies which operate in the region – Hamersley Iron, Cliffs Robe River Iron Associates, Goldsworthy Mining Company, Woodside Petroleum – have invested over $2 billion establishing major mines at Mount Tom Price, Paraburdoo, Shay Gap, Newman, Pannawonica, and Goldsworthy, constructing 10 new towns, building 1,200 kilometres of private railways, developing and expanding five ports and completing two pelletising plants. The sand dunes, particularly at the southern end of the Pilbara, are huge and seemingly endless, set over a kilometre apart and rising up to 15 metres above the surrounding land. The gorges of the Hamersley Range National Park are recognised as one of the most dramatic areas in Australia.

At the top of Western Australia is the Kimberley, a vast wonderland of desert scenery equalling the MacDonnell Ranges in Central Australia. Tourist brochures proudly announce the Kimberley as being 'three times the size of England'. It is here that the dramatic Bungle Bungle Ranges, with their strange horizontal bedding, await the traveller prepared to drive over one of the worst roads on the continent – 100 kilometres in four hours and that is if you don't break an axle! The infamous Gibb River Road offers a road so bad that at either end you can buy car stickers which read 'I survived the Gibb River Road' – the 'I' referring to both the passengers and the car! The 646-kilometre-long dirt road (there are 62 kilometres of sealed road at the Derby end) passes through places as Rollie's Jump Up, Bluey O'Malley's Crossing, Windjana Gorge and Penguin Road.

This is the region of dramatic lookouts, vast floodplains, dramatic sandstone and quartzite formations, a spectacular fossilised coral reef which appears and disappears into the landscape, emerging as a dramatic limestone range, and of the ubiquitous boab or baobab tree. The area has experienced a major tourist boom in recent years. This is best symbolised by Lord McAlpine's $55 million development at Cable Beach, the sealing of the road from Port Hedland to the Northern Territory border (which means that the region is now accessible to all vehicles in the dry season), and the number of tourist operators who vie for business on trips to the Bungle Bungles, Lake Argyle and the gorges on the Gibb River Road.

Although access to the Bungle Bungle Ranges (below) in the Kimberley region of Western Australia is very difficult, there is more than enough to reward travellers venturing into this area.

Beyond Perth lies the great wheatbelt of Western Australia. For hundreds of kilometres the landscape is an endless sea of wheatfields and the small towns, servicing the surrounding area, are nothing more than a single pub, a farm machinery sales centre, a general store, a council building and a few dozen houses.

NEW SOUTH WALES

NEW SOUTH WALES is the hub of Australia. Not only is it the state with the largest capital city and the largest population, but it also has the most memorable of the country's man-made symbols, notably the magnificent Sydney Harbour Bridge and the Opera House with its graceful white sails. Located on the Harbour, Sydney has long been acclaimed as one of the most beautiful cities in the world. There are world-famous beaches close by, and hundreds of kilometres of coastline with seemingly endless, sandy beaches stretch along the state's eastern seaboard. Beyond the coast lies the Great Dividing Range with the rugged mountains of the New England area and the spectacular gorges of the Blue Mountains. To the west the state becomes drier and flatter as the greenness of the coastal plains and the mountains gives way to the vast plains which slowly degenerate into an unforgiving desert landscape. The state's city dwellers could easily forget that beyond the mountains, which form a natural barrier, lies an ancient land, worn flat by time, where graziers fight for survival against the constant threat of drought and where, for thousands of years before the arrival of Europeans, Aborigines lived a simple life, celebrating their closeness to the land by painting their Dreamtime in the dry, dusty caves of the outback.

Sydney (left) has a population of over 3.7 million people and one of the finest harbours in the world, with a typically modern skyline where huge multi-storey office complexes reach heavenward. During the past 30 years, the face of the city centre has changed dramatically – in the 1960s only a few buildings, near Circular Quay, were more than ten storeys high!

The Opera House (left), with its dramatic white sails, has become one of Sydney's most distinctive symbols. Designed by the gifted Danish architect, Joern Utzon, it cost over $100 million by the time it was completed in 1973. It is hard to believe that this impressive building was once little more than an imaginative sketch. Major problems had to be overcome during its construction and, although Utzon eventually resigned from the project, the Opera House remains a monument to a great imagination. Today its four theatres and attractive walkways offer locals and visitors a range of interesting activities.

The Harbour Bridge (below), premier icon of Sydney and one of the largest single-span bridges in the world, was finally completed in 1932 after nine years' work. Known affectionately as 'The Coathanger' and simply 'The Bridge', the main span is 503 metres long, with the top of the arch rising 134 metres above sea level. The bridge cost £9,577,507 to construct.

Before completion of the Harbour Bridge (opposite), Sydney could boast one of the most extensive ferry services in the world. Effectively, the southern and northern suburbs were cut off from each other, unless you were prepared to travel to the western suburbs and then cross the Parramatta River. Today the bridge, seen here at its southern end from Miller's Point, and the harbour tunnel are vital links between the northern and southern parts of the city.

The Opera House and the Harbour Bridge (previous pages), Sydney's best-known symbols, are separated by Circular Quay. These two structures are situated at the heart of the city, the one representing its cultural centre, the other its most important transport link.

Excellent seafood restaurants abound in Sydney. Few are more widely known or admired than Doyles (below) at Watsons Bay. Offering superb harbour views from its tables, and providing plates laden with the latest catch as well as some of the country's most prized crustaceans, it is one of the most popular eateries in the city, and justifiably so.

A monument to Captain Arthur Phillip (opposite) has an appropriate place in Sydney's Botanic Gardens, near where he established the infant colony of New South Wales in 1788. Phillip explored the harbour foreshores and decided that Sydney Cove would be a suitable site for a convict settlement. His statue gazes out across the city he created.

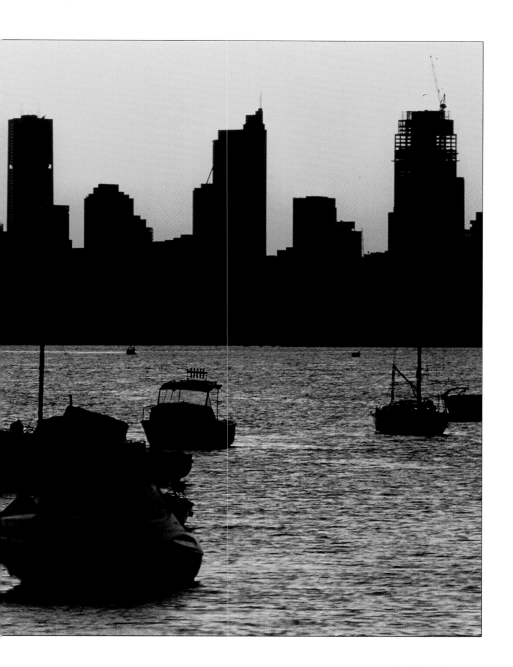

Sydney Harbour (left) is extraordinary from all angles. On a summer's day, sailing boats scud across the water, while the people of Sydney relax in a park or on a beach at the harbourside, walking, picnicking or swimming. A special feature of Watsons Bay is that visitors can enjoy both a splendid view across the harbour and a dramatic vista of the Pacific Ocean.

Darling Harbour (opposite, bottom) is the most recent tourist development in Sydney. Covering 54 hectares and costing an estimated $1,800 million, it is similar to the Fisherman's Wharf in San Francisco. It boasts an amusement park, a wide variety of specialist and gift shops, and the city's most prestigious conference centre. Darling Harbour has many other drawcards, such as street theatre, access to the harbour by ferry, and excellent restaurants with pleasant harbour views.

The Lord Nelson Hotel (below), Sydney's oldest continuously licensed hotel, was built in 1834 when the Rocks was a rough-and-ready area full of criminals, sailors and ex-convicts. Originally the hotel was built as a two-storey domestic residence with verandahs. In 1842 it was granted its first licence. Since then it has become one of Sydney's most popular and historic watering holes.

On 21 January 1788 Captain Arthur Phillip sailed up the coast from Botany Bay and entered Sydney Harbour. The first landing place within Port Jackson was Camp Cove (left), an attractive small bay near the harbour's South Head. Today this historic site where the first Europeans stepped ashore is one more vantage point where the beauty of the harbour can be appreciated.

The Archibald Fountain (above), one of Sydney's best-known monuments, stands in Hyde Park at the top of the historic Macquarie Street. The fountain was completed in 1932. Its original purpose, to commemorate the association of France and Australia during World War I, has been forgotten by most Sydneysiders who see it as a pleasant meeting place for those who wish to enjoy a picnic lunch in the park.

Bondi Beach has, despite Sydney's attractive necklace of rival beaches stretching nearly 80 kilometres from Palm Beach in the north to Cronulla in the south, retained its standing as the most famous of all. Equally renowned are the bronzed Bondi Life-savers (left), who have come to symbolise the healthy, active and sun-loving image of Australians.

Rugby League is one of Sydney's great sporting passions. Each winter teams compete for the coveted Winfield Cup. The grand final is always held at the Sydney Football Stadium (bottom left), an elegant, modern building designed in the form of a huge bowl. In recent times the venue has also been used for rock concerts.

Australians are obsessed with sports. To leave work early, get a few cans of beer, and head to the Sydney Cricket Ground (right) to watch a fast and furious, 50-overs-a-side day-night match is, for many people, about as close to heaven as they could ever hope for. If that match happens to be against one of the traditional adversaries – England or the West Indies – and, even better, if Australia wins, there is cause for real celebration!

The cliffs of North Head (left), with views from Fairfax Lookout and the Walkway, offer visitors spectacular vistas across the harbour. Nearby is the Quarantine Station, which started operations in 1832. North Head is one of two headlands which protect Sydney Harbour from the Pacific Ocean, allowing only a narrow opening into the harbour.

To the north of Sydney lies the magnificent Ku-ring-gai Chase National Park with its northern border on Broken Bay. Bobbin Head (below) is the most developed area of the park, with the famous Halvorsen Boat Sheds (and a variety of other nautical organisations) offering cruisers for hire. The peacefulness of the area attracts enthusiastic sailors for weekend jaunts or longer holidays, spent exploring the reaches of the bay and the Hawkesbury River.

Bondi (left), like Waikiki, San Tropez and Malibu, is one of the world's most famous beaches, but partly owes it fame to the fact that it is close to the centre of Sydney. Although few people regard it as Sydney's best beach, this does not stop crowds of up to 25,000 arriving here during the summer months. Recently Bondi has acquired a cosmopolitan air, and thousands of English tourists flock there on Christmas Day to celebrate the holiday.

Bondi is renowned for its life-savers, which is hardly surprising because its Life-saving Club dates back to 1906. Some of the most dramatic rescue acts have occurred off the beach, and the image of a boat carving its way through the surf, with life-savers heaving on the oars (below), has been a great source of relief to people caught in a rip and being dragged out to sea. It is common to see the life-savers in action during one of the summer surf carnivals.

The Gap (left) is a dramatic indentation in the cliffs just to the south of Sydney's South Head. In 1857 it became the site of one of the most famous shipwrecks of the nineteenth century when the *Dunbar*, mistaking The Gap for The Heads, crashed into the coast with the loss of 121 lives. For many years it had a reputation as a place for suicides (a rather unusual claim to fame), but nowadays it is recognised as one of the best lookouts across the Pacific Ocean.

Jervis Bay (above), unlike most of the coast south of Sydney, is not an area noted for its surf. It is characterised by gently sloping, sandy beaches, rocky headlands which are easy to walk around, and quiet places where family picnics seem to be the most natural thing in the world. But most of all, it is the beaches — impossibly white, breathtakingly beautiful and remarkably peaceful — and the bushwalks which hold so much appeal for visitors to this largely unspoiled area.

Echo Point (left) is a perfect
starting point for any visit to the
Blue Mountains. This superb lookout, located near Katoomba, offers
exceptional views of Mount Solitary,
the Three Sisters (especially when
lit at night), the Ruined Castle and
the vast Jamieson Valley.

The Blue Mountains consist
of a series of box canyons where
the water from the ridges tumbles
down sheer cliffs and through
quiet valleys. At Wentworth Falls,
a bushwalk leads from the picnic
area at the Valley of the Waters to
the Empress Falls (above), which
plunge over the cliff to join the
Jamieson Valley far below.

The area around Broken Hill (opposite), one of Australia's great mining towns, has become so famous that it is now regularly featured in movies. Ironically, many of the inhabitants of New South Wales have never been beyond the Great Dividing Range, and few realise that the western half of their state is harsh and dry. Here the land is marginal, droughts may destroy a flock of sheep, and people have to be tough to survive.

The great Darling River system (above) expands into a series of vast lakes near the tiny township of Menindee. Most of these lakes form part of the Kinchega National Park. In a land so arid and forbidding, it is extraordinary to come across extensive areas of water surrounded by saltbush and inhospitable red soils, with colonies of waterbirds such as black swans, herons and ibises living beside them.

Tibooburra (right), situated some 1,500 kilometres from Sydney and 183 metres above sea level, is known to most people in New South Wales as the 'hottest town' in the state. Although it is also its most isolated town, the adventure of the outback – the desire to return to an Australia which has all but disappeared – ensures that visitors make their way there. Tibooburra probably means 'pile of granite rocks' in the language of the local Aborigines; a number of the granite outcrops near the town are regarded as sacred sites of mythological and religious significance.

CAMERONS CORNER
IN 1882-83 SURVEYOR JOHN CAMERON WAS IN CHARGE OF THE TEAM THAT COMPLETED THE FIRST BOUNDARY SURVEY
BETWEEN N.S.W. AND QLD. HE PLANNED TO BUILD A CAIRN HERE BUT A SHORTAGE OF STONE FORCED HIM TO ERECT A
A PEG INSTEAD. THIS PEG IS NOW ON DISPLAY IN TIBOOBURRA.

The Sturt National Park (previous pages) covers 295,189 hectares of classic outback terrain. With less than 200 millimetres of rain a year, the scenery ranges from red sand dunes to gibber plains and 'jump-up' country – isolated mesas which rise forlornly above their flat surroundings. The flora of the park consists mostly of mulga bushland and arid scrubland inhabited by kangaroos, euros and a large variety of lizards and birds, including the wedge-tailed eagle and pink galah.

Cameron's Corner (left) is where New South Wales, Queensland and South Australia meet. The dingo fence (the longest construction on earth) runs through the area. It is estimated that between 1880 and 1910 more than 50 per cent of all the wildlife in the region was driven from the land by greedy graziers who overstocked it to a point where most of the edible saltbush and copper-burr was destroyed.

With about two-thirds of Australia receiving less than 250 millimetres of rain annually, and the continent boasting a dry, desert area second only to the Sahara, it is hardly surprising that outback graziers and stockmen constantly have to fight the drought-ravaged land, trying to keep their animals alive in country which is at best marginal and at worst little more than hot, scrubby desert (opposite, top).

The Wagga Wagga Post Office (opposite, bottom) is a fine example of a late-Victorian, Classical Revival building, and is a typical medium-sized country post office of the period. Along with the Court House and the CBC Bank, it is one of a series of nineteenth-century buildings which make Wagga Wagga's Fitzmaurice Street a showpiece of rural New South Wales architecture.

Most Aboriginal art expresses a love of the land and its inhabitants. The Aboriginal art of painting and engraving kangaroos, wallabies, birds and emus (left) is known to be the most ancient artistic expression on earth. Long before the first Europeans were painting on the walls of caves in southern France and Spain, Aborigines had developed cave art to a high level of sophistication. Some of the most impressive examples of their art are found in the far western Mootwingee National Park, above Amphitheatre Gorge. These hand stencils (middle left), produced by blowing paint over a hand placed on a rock, are typical of the rich variety of work on display in the region. Aborigines have lived in this area for over 30,000 years. Congregating beside the billabongs and creek beds, the cliffs became their art gallery. Also to be found in Mootwingee National Park are petrographs of the 'crack men' (bottom left), located on the cliffs above Homestead Creek.

The area beyond Broken Hill (right) was called 'the great grey plain' by the Australian author, Henry Lawson. It is a region where saltbush takes over before the red sand dunes finally conquer everything. For most people in New South Wales, the town is no more than a mining community on the edge of the desert. This is particularly true for those who drive beyond to the ghost town of Silverton. Here, where the movie *Mad Max 2* was made, the scrub and red soils seem to go on forever.

Even when Lord Howe Island (left) is bathed in sunshine, it is quite common to see the peaks of Mount Gower and Mount Lidgbird, rising respectively 875 metres and 777 metres above sea level, hidden by mist. These two summits tower over the 11-kilometre-long island which lies about 700 kilometres northeast of Sydney.

The kentia palm tree (above), widely cultivated as an ornamental plant, is one of 57 species of vegetation native to Lord Howe Island. It mixes freely with a large number of species, such as the banyan tree, from neighbouring land masses. The flora and fauna of Lord Howe Island differ significantly from those of the mainland.

The superb new Parliament House (above) in Canberra was built in 1988 on Capital Hill and overlooks Lake Burley Griffin. Designed so that visitors can walk on top of the building, it boasts an excellent art gallery and facilities which feature a wide range of Australian timbers. The first parliament house was completed in 1927 and was the hub of the nation's political life for 61 years.

Canberra, the national capital, is a carefully designed city of circuits and long, elegant roads. In the middle of the city is the artificial Lake Burley Griffin (opposite, bottom), named after the city's town planner, and surrounded by important buildings such as the National Library and High Court. One of the highlights of the lake is the Cook waterjet which, most days, shoots water high above the lake.

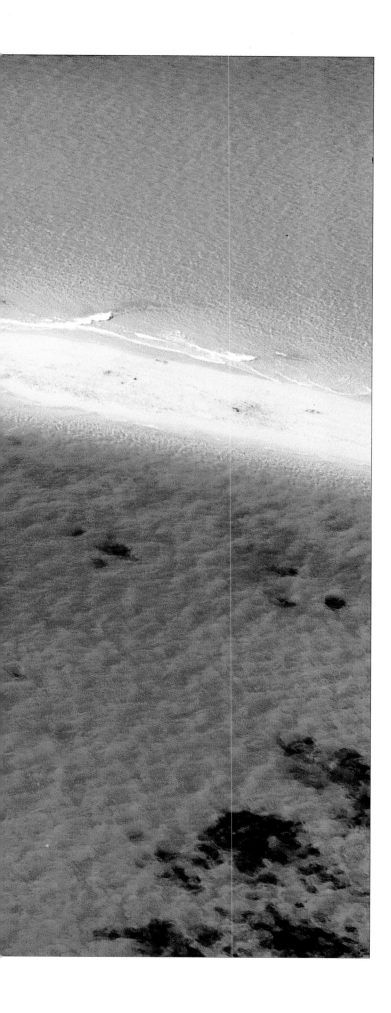

QUEENSLAND

IT IS NO WONDER that most visitors to
Australia nominate Queensland as their
premier destination, lapped as it is
by tropical waters and boasting the
Great Barrier Reef, one of the natural
wonders of the world. Queensland
claims that it has been blessed with
perfect weather — its warm winters and
long, hot summers have acted like a
magnet for people from the southern states eager to get
a little sunshine in their lives. This 'perfect' weather has
led to a statewide ambience of informality and relaxation.
It doesn't matter whether you're lying on a beach of the
Gold Coast, soaking up the sun in the exclusive resorts
around Noosa Heads, scudding across the northern
Queensland reefs in a pleasure craft, or snorkelling and
marvelling at the tropical fish and the myriad coloured
corals, Queensland has something for even the most
demanding visitor. Beyond the coast lies the Great
Dividing Range with its numerous waterfalls and deep,
silent gorges where tropical ferns and moss abound.
Further west is the Artesian Basin where bores bring hot
waters from hundreds of metres below the surface to wet
the parched, near-desert lands. This is marginal country
where hardy graziers eke a living from the unforgiving soil.

The waters off the north Queensland coast (left) seem to
belong more to picture postcards than to the real world. The white
coral sands turn the coastal waters into a shimmering green and
beyond the shoreline, the colours change to ever-deepening shades
of blue. No wonder Cairns has recently become the most popular
tourist destination in north Queensland.

Brisbane (top) is Australia's third largest city, with a population of about 1.3 million people. Today soaring high-rise buildings characterise the sophisticated, urbane state capital on the banks of the Brisbane River. There was a time, only 30 years ago, when it was little more than a large country town.

Brisbane can boast one of the finest cultural complexes (above) in Australia. Opened to coincide with the Brisbane World Expo in 1988, the South Bank complex includes the Queensland Art Gallery, the imposing Performing Arts Complex, the Queensland Museum and the State Library. Located across the Victoria Bridge from the city's central business district, it was designed by a local architect, Robin Gibson, and has successfully drawn together, on the banks of the Brisbane River, most of the city's major cultural activities.

Surfers Paradise is at the heart of the Gold Coast. Located 83 kilometres south of Brisbane, Surfers Paradise and its beach (right) symbolise the lifestyle and aspirations of the people who come to the area to holiday or to live. But it is far more than just a sunny destination – true to its name, it really is a 'paradise for surfers'. Few visitors realise that beyond the narrow coastal plain lies a cool and peaceful mountain range noted for its tea rooms and gift shops – a far cry from the vibrancy of the coast.

In the past 20 years, ports and resorts have developed rapidly along the Queensland coast. In the 1950s Mooloolaba (left) was little more than a few excellent beaches and many sand dunes. Today it has a thriving fishing and prawning fleet. The area is noted for the pleasure craft moored near the mouth of the Mooloolah River.

Maroochydore (above) is a classic Queensland holiday destination in the heart of the Sunshine Coast. It owes its popularity to kilometres of golden beaches, pleasant beach parks, small shopping centres geared to tourists and a relaxed atmosphere all year round. This is where people go to play golf and tennis, to surf or just to relax on a beach and soak up the sun.

The Lamington National Park (opposite) is a popular retreat for Brisbane residents who find the cool rainforest, 600 metres above the sea, a welcome respite from the summer humidity of the city. The rainforest is rich in elkhorns, orchids and ferns, and offers the visitor a wide range of walking paths.

Fraser Island (above), the largest sand island in the world, was the scene of shipwrecks throughout the nineteenth century. Of the many places of interest here, the site of the wreck of the *Maheno* is one of the most popular. After 30 years of service in Australian waters, the *Maheno* was being towed to Japan as scrap when it hit cyclonic conditions off the coast and was washed ashore on 9 July 1935.

This road through Pile Valley (right) on Fraser Island is typical of the tropical beauty which awaits the visitor. There is also Woongoolbver Creek, which carries clear water through the island's rainforest; Lake Wabby, the island's deepest lake, which is rich in fish and surrounded by ancient melaleucas; and Rainbow Gorge with its coloured sand formations.

Noosa (previous pages), on the Queensland coast, has become one of the country's premier upmarket destinations. The Noosa National Park, located on the headland beyond Little Cove, is a small coastal park in which birds and small mammals find refuge in the native flora. The bushwalks and picnic spots stand in sharp contrast to the urbanity of the nearby Noosa shopping centre.

The delightful Curtis Falls (below) are found on the road from North Tambourine to Beaudesert.

The Tambourine mountain region has much to offer the visitor, including beautiful views on both sides of the mountain range and a number of rainforest areas with quiet streams and waterfalls.

Toompine (bottom) can be reached on a less-than-perfect dirt road, some 77 kilometres to the south of the tiny outback town of Quilpie. Once a stopping point for the western Queensland Cobb & Co mail and passenger services, and the centre of a thriving mining community, it is now nothing

more than the Toompine Hotel, a solitary pub built in 1898 to meet the needs of the area.

Lake Moogerah (right), a popular haunt for water-skiers and boating enthusiasts, is located just over 80 kilometres to the southwest of Brisbane near the town of Boonah. Nearby are the Mount French and Moogerah Peaks national parks. The latter has a number of volcanic peaks and rocky cliffs, while the climb to the top of Mount French is rewarded by panoramic views over the Fassifern Valley.

Lying behind the Gold Coast is a beautiful escarpment which rises to a series of small villages, offering a respite from the commercialisation and bustle of the coast. On the road between Murwillumbah and Nerang, the Natural Arch National Park (above), is a place of cool valleys, rushing streams and some extra-ordinary rock formations. This is a side of the Gold Coast rarely seen by visitors.

The Romavale Winery (opposite, top), on the Injune Road outside Roma, can claim to be the oldest winery in Queensland. It started operations in 1863 and has been producing wine continuously for over a century. At one point, the present cellars were processing grapes from 170,000 vines. Grape-growing and wine-making is part of Roma's history: the first vines in the area were planted at Mt Abundance Homestead in the late 1840s, and by the early 1870s wine-making was an important local industry.

The Jondaryan Woolshed Historical Museum (opposite, bottom) is an outstanding example of local enthusiasm and enterprise. In 1972 it was decided to use the Woolshed as the centrepiece of a park which would become a 'living memorial to the historic pastoral industry and the pioneers of rural Australia'. Today it is an important tourist attraction, comprising a large number of buildings, but the centrepiece is the Woolshed itself. At Jondaryan, the highlight of each year is the nine-day Australian Heritage Festival, held at the end of August. During the festival, people come from all over the country to display traditional bushcrafts. At this time, the machinery in this remarkable museum complex becomes operational.

The city of Caloundra (opposite) is the most southerly resort on the famed Sunshine Coast. With its 13 kilometres of delightful beaches such as Curramundi, Kings, Moffatt, Shelly, Dicky, Bulcock and Golden Beach, and its greenery, its near-perfect climate and easy lifestyle, it attracts young commuters, holiday-makers and retired people alike. On any morning, in the narrow strait between Caloundra and the northern tip of Bribie Island, there are people fishing for their breakfast, or maybe their lunch or dinner. Caloundra is that kind of place. No wonder most sources claim that the Aboriginal word 'callanda' meant 'beautiful' or 'beautiful place'.

Beyond the Great Dividing Range, Queensland (above) becomes a vast and dry semi-desert where the roads are impossibly straight and the visitor can travel up to 200 kilometres between towns, seeing only the occasional passing car and kangaroo. This is the true outback where the skies are perfectly blue and the sense of loneliness and isolation is overwhelming.

The Warwick Town Hall (right) was constructed of local sandstone in 1888. It is one of the oldest local authority buildings in the state and is distinguished by its clock tower. Over the years it has played host to a variety of entertainments. In 1900 the mayor stood on the balcony and called for cheers for Colonel Baden-Powell to celebrate the news of the relief of Mafeking; in 1908 a Biograph company showed movies in the hall; Peter Dawson performed there in 1914 and in 1952 Sister Kenny was the acclaimed guest at the Anzac Day celebrations.

The Queen Mary Falls National Park lies 10 kilometres from Killarney. On the way up are the Browns Falls, where visitors can clamber in behind the falling water, and the 38-metre Dagg's Falls. The Queen Mary Falls (opposite), dropping a spectacular 40 metres into a rainforest gorge, form part of the park. Carr's Lookout, eight kilometres further on, provides excellent views of the upper reaches of the Condamine River, the start of Australia's longest river system.

Some of the most attractive railway stations in Australia are to be found in Queensland. For years the picturesque railway station at Kuranda, a beautiful small town inland from Cairns, was a popular place for tourists because of its magnificent floral displays. Similarly, the Spring Bluff Railway Station (above) greets visitors with verdant gardens, recalling a time when the railway was the vital transport link throughout Queensland.

Small boats depart regularly from Cairns and Port Douglas, taking tourists through the crystal-clear water of the Great Barrier Reef to offshore destinations such as the beautiful Lady Musgrave Island (left).

Dunk Island's (above) most famous resident, Edmund James Banfield, once wrote: 'In these calm and shallow waters there is a never-ending panorama of entertainment. Coral gardens – gardens of the sea nymphs, wherein fancy feigns cool, shy, chaste faces and pliant forms half-revealed among gently swaying robes; a company of porpoises, a herd of dugong; turtle, queer and familiar fish'.

Hamilton Island (left), one of the most luxurious resort destinations on the Great Barrier Reef, has hotel suites, private villas, luxury apartments, six pools, a swimming pool bar and this luxury marina, which can provide moorings for 200 boats. The island also has the Mountain Top Fauna Park with koalas, emus, kangaroos and wombats, and a church for holiday weddings.

The Great Barrier Reef is one of Australia's great tourist attractions and one of the wonders of the world. People come from everywhere to watch the whales, to marvel at the multicoloured coral displays, to stare through glass-bottomed boats at the exotic and richly coloured tropical fish, and to go snorkelling (opposite) on the reef where fish and coral surround the visitors.

V ICTORIA

VICTORIA, the smallest of the mainland
states, is an area of remarkable diversity.
At its heart lies the sophisticated and
charming southern city of Melbourne
with its wide streets and elegant
Victorian buildings, all of which
reflect the city's boom era during the
goldrush of the late-nineteenth century.
Victoria proudly declares itself to be 'The
Garden State', and no matter which way the roads lead
from Melbourne, this is true. The beautiful Dandenong
Ranges to the east of the capital are characterised by
tall gum trees and quiet settlements in sleepy valleys.
To the north and west, the rich soils, extensive grasslands
and good rainfall are a perfect combination for sheep
and cattle grazing, the nurturing of vineyards, and for
the growing of a wide range of other crops. To the south
lies one of the wonders of Australia – the Great Ocean
Road. Winding for 320 kilometres along the coastline,
it reveals small, intimate beaches, spectacular headlands
and, to the far west, the rugged limestone cliffs around
Port Campbell, where the unrelenting fury of the
Southern Ocean has worn away the coastline to form
islands of rock like the Twelve Apostles. Inland, many
of the state's towns bear witness to the goldrush. Solid
Victorian buildings, the remnants of gold diggings, and
marvellous evocations of a bustling quest for riches can
be seen from Ballarat to Beechworth, and from Bendigo
to the lovely town of Bright.

The Twelve Apostles (left), a series of 12 stone islands near
Port Campbell, are regarded as the highlight of any journey along
the Great Ocean Road in Victoria. This 320-kilometre road winds
along the southwestern coastline of the state, offering the visitor
dramatic cliffs, attractive seaside resorts and unusual seascapes.

The Yarra (left) was once described, albeit unfairly, as the only river which flowed upside down. The river, which is mostly brown and muddy, runs through the heart of Melbourne. Its banks offer excellent parks and interesting vantage points. At the magical moments of sunrise and sunset, the views across the river will persuade even the sternest critic that this body of water holds great charm.

Captain Cook's cottage (above), transported in 1934 from Great Ayton in Yorkshire and re-erected in the grounds of King's Domain Gardens to celebrate Melbourne's centenary, is a tangible celebration of the first European to sail up the east coast of Australia. The ivy on the walls was grown from a cutting taken from the cottage in 1934 before it was removed.

Although trams (right) are long gone from Sydney, and there is only a token tram left in Adelaide, they are still part of the fabric of Melbourne. This tram travels up Collins Street, noted for its arcades, boutiques and luxury goods shops.

The city of Melbourne (opposite) is justifiably famous for its street cafés and restaurants. It is said that the large number of Italians who migrated to Melbourne in the 1950s brought their café society with them. Certainly Melbourne is proud of its multiculturalism, and the urbanity of its street life and café society makes the city a very special place.

The Mount Buffalo National Park (above) lies 320 kilometres northeast of Melbourne. It is a dramatic granite plateau with 140 kilometres of walking trails which lead beside icy mountain streams, spectacular gorges and twisted snow gums to several lookouts. This early morning view from below Bent's Lookout is typical of the scenery in the park.

Rutherglen, Victoria's premier wine town, is surrounded by vineyards which produce grapes for a range of reds and whites. The Jolimont Winery (above left), established in 1886 and refurbished and reopened a century later, boasts an excellent restaurant as well as a monthly food and craft market. It is one of the newest wineries in the valley, but the historical character of the setting has been maintained.

Chambers Rosewood Winery (above right), just to the north of Rutherglen, has been in the hands of the same family for nearly 125 years. In 1870 William Chambers bought a vineyard noted for its fortified wines from Anthony Ruche. Today the winery is owned by Bill Chambers, the great grandson of the original purchaser.

Known as the Grape Vine Hotel or Star Hotel (opposite, bottom), this complex in the main street of Chiltern once included a hotel as well as the Star Theatre, a billiard room and stables. Built by the company of Crawford and Connelly, the theatre provided entertainment for the goldminers who flocked to the town. At times it presented vaudeville performances, plays and dances.

The Wandiligong Valley (above), located southeast of the township of Bright, is famous for its rich soils. It is here that both tobacco and apples are grown; one of the local apple orchards is reputed to be the largest in the southern hemisphere. The valley has been classified by the National Trust.

The Chinese cemetery (left) in Beechworth is one of this perfectly preserved mining town's many attractions. Dating from the 1850s, the cemetery includes the Chinese Burning Towers and an altar,

which were used to send offerings to souls of deceased Chinese miners. There are more than 500 miners' graves in the cemetery.

It is said that the Chateau Tahbilk Winery (opposite), eight kilometres south of Nagambie, was named after an Aboriginal expression meaning 'the place of many waters'. Established in 1860 on the river, the winery is noted for its superb old cellars, its unusual tiered belfry and its old mulberry trees. The winery specialises in a wide range of unfortified wines.

Gold was discovered at Spring Creek, near the present site of Beechworth (above), in 1852. Within months the town was teeming with prospectors. The mining community disappeared long ago, but the town has maintained its heritage, with over 30 buildings being classified by the National Trust. An active conservation and restoration policy has done much to restore the town to its former glory.

Lake Eildon (right) was built during the 1950s to generate hydro-electricity for Victoria. It is the largest artificial lake in the state and, as such, has become a popular tourist resort. Located on the edge of the Snowy Mountains, the wall of the dam offers excellent views while the dam itself has boat harbours and launching ramps, as well as a number of attractive picnic spots.

TASMANIA

TASMANIA is like no other Australian state. Separated from the dry mainland by Bass Strait and buffeted by the cold winds which blow off the Southern Ocean, it is wet, intimate and intensely European. It was here, in the early nineteenth century, that convicts worked from dawn to dark to cut timber and build prisons at Port Arthur and Macquarie Harbour. The state capital, Hobart, has a unique charm. Beautiful Victorian houses and cottages nestle along the shores of the Derwent. The city seems to gravitate around the harbour and the elegant Salamanca Place where old warehouses have been turned into gift and craft shops and where, each weekend, the famous Salamanca Market takes place. To the north of Hobart several beautifully preserved nineteenth-century villages such as Richmond, Ross, Oatlands and Campbell Town sit astride the road between the capital and the northern city of Launceston. To the west the wild and rugged ranges, with the impressive Cradle Mountain and a large number of glacial lakes, offer bushwalkers and hikers tracks and scenery far removed from the dryness and flatness which characterise most of the Australian mainland.

The appeal of Coles Bay (left) and Freycinet National Park is that they haven't really changed in 50 years. Today people come to the area to fish in the waters of Great Oyster Bay, to walk in the park, or to climb the Hazards and the mountains to the south, both of which offer marvellous views across the bay and the Tasman Sea. This area is alive with unusual animals – Tasmanian pademelons, white-breasted sea eagles and red-necked wallabies. In season, Coles Bay's attractions include spectacular displays of rare native flora.

Hobart (left) lies on either side of the Derwent River and is partially protected by Mount Wellington in the west, which dominates the landscape from a height of 1,270 metres, and Mount Nelson to the south. This dramatic landscape results in a series of microclimates, producing considerable variations within the city. Hobart's western suburbs experience more rain and the southern suburbs have mild onshore breezes in summer.

By 1850 Battery Point had become the marine focal point of Hobart. Sailors from all over the world came to the area, and sailors' and workers' cottages were built in a place already noted for its gracious Georgian mansions. These neat, tiny cottages (above), once owned by working people, stand next to stately homes in streetscapes which include narrow, winding roads and 'village greens'.

The coast around Bicheno
(above) is famous for its unusual
and dramatic formations. The
coastline includes an impressive
local blowhole and the famous
Rocking Rock, a huge 80-ton piece
of granite, balanced so that it rocks
with the movement of the tide. Be
careful – in the right conditions
you can easily get soaked by an
unexpected wave! There are a
number of access points to the rocks
which have a distinctive red colour
as a result of red lichen deposits.

**The docks and Salamanca
Place** (right) are at the heart of
Hobart. It is here that, every year,
the victorious yacht which has
led the fleet from Sydney to Hobart
arrives. It is here that, each weekend, locals and visitors meet and
mingle in the excellent Salamanca
Markets. And it is here that old
Georgian warehouses have been
converted into excellent restaurants,
galleries, and craft and gift shops.

Strahan (previous pages), a small fishing and tourist township, is located on the edge of the unspoiled Macquarie Harbour, the last outpost of civilisation on the Tasmanian west coast and surely one of the loneliest places on earth. The British created this place as the ultimate penal colony. Macquarie Harbour is 50 kilometres long and opens to the sea through the narrow, eddying waters of Hell's Gates. Popular harbour cruises offer scenic views of the countryside.

The walks in the Freycinet National Park (above) are noted for their spectacular coastal scenery. As a brochure on the area declares: 'Where else would you find granite mountains rising straight from the sea to form a magnificent sheltered waterway? Where else would you find a beach so beautiful and secluded that on the last Royal visit to Australia, the Royal Yacht Britannia anchored to allow the Queen ashore for an Australian-style beach barbecue?'

In 1982 the Cradle Mountain-Lake St Clair National Park was placed on the world heritage list in recognition of its outstanding natural, cultural and wilderness qualities. Today this lovely area is a model of an accessible wilderness region, with numerous huts and a wide range of walks through the mountains. Nothing quite compares with the beauty which awaits visitors who take the road to the edges of Lake Dove (right) in the shadow of Cradle Mountain.

Tasmania is dotted with deserted buildings which reflect the changing circumstances of the state. It has always relied upon agriculture and primary industries to sustain it, and since its settlement in the early nineteenth century, it has seen recessions and depressions take a harsh toll on its population. An abandoned barn, like this one near Meander (left), may look appealing but it tells a story of rural hardship.

The Liffey Falls (above) is a series of three cascades set among luxuriant ferns in a eucalypt rainforest, just 24 kilometres to the south of the country town of Deloraine. The falls offer a cool retreat combined with an excellent picnic ground, and are typical of the area, where the Meander and Montana Falls also provide visitors with fine walks and magnificent scenery.

Launceston (left) is Tasmania's major northern port. The boats in the harbour remind visitors seduced by the architectural beauties of the city that both pleasure and trading craft have moored at Launceston from the early nineteenth century.

Ross is one of the most perfectly preserved nineteenth-century towns in Australia. The main highway from Hobart to Launceston bypasses the town, leaving the tidy cottages, beautiful churches such as Uniting Church (below) and one of the oldest bridges (right) in Australia intact. Built by convicts in 1836, the crossing is a perfect vantage point for admiring the quaint, rather English charm of the village with its meadows running down to the Macquarie River.

SOUTH AUSTRALIA

MORE THAN HALF OF SOUTH AUSTRALIA consists of desert. Beyond Port Augusta, at the northern end of the Spencer Gulf, the traveller enters a world of mesas, sand dunes, salt lakes, blisteringly hot days and very cold nights. To the south of the deserts, the winter rains and the ever-improving soils have made South Australia the wine and citrus centre of the country. To the south of the beautiful Flinders Ranges – a range of red soils, white ghost gums and blue skies – lie the fertile Clare and Barossa valleys where some of Australia's finest grapes are grown and finest wines are fermented. Further east, the Murray River valley is ideal for growing oranges, mandarins, grapefruit and other lesser-known varieties of citrus fruit. But for all this richness, it is the area around the state capital, Adelaide, which captures the imagination of the visitor. Tiny villages with opulent houses nestle close to the Adelaide Hills and offer some of the best restaurants and craft shops in the country. Adelaide itself, the gracious 'city of churches' on the banks of the Torrens, has the charm of a country town and the elegance of a great city. To the south of the city the coastline, including the wildlife refuge of Kangaroo Island with its sandy beaches and sea lions, and the long, white strip known as The Coorong, have been largely untouched by modern development.

A statue of John McDouall Stuart (left), the man who successfully crossed the continent from South Australia to the present site of Darwin, overlooks Victoria Square in Adelaide.

Everyone who visits Adelaide (above left) is left with lasting images of the city, the slow-flowing River Torrens, the parks and, inevitably, the churches. Dubbed 'the city of churches', it is more the serenity of the city than the number of churches which conjures up this notion of religious commitment. The image of rowers on the Torrens is a reminder that Adelaide has a sense of elegance and Englishness.

At night many of Adelaide's most attractive buildings are lit up, taking on a completely different look. The old Adelaide Railway Station (opposite, below) is an outstanding example of late nineteenth-century architecture, and, along with the Parliament House and the Constitutional Museum, forms an impressive run of buildings from King William Street down North Terrace.

The National Soldiers Memorial (above) in Adelaide commemorates those South Australians who gave their lives for their country in the wars since Federation. The city's monuments include the war memorial, representing the prologue and epilogue to war, and the marvellous bronze equestrian statue which stands as a reminder to the South Australians who fell in the South African campaign.

Victoria Square (above), an area of just over 3.2 hectares in the centre of Adelaide, was laid out by Colonel Light in 1837. The square is notable for its attractive modern fountain, the fine buildings surrounding it, and the grassy areas and trees that provide a convenient meeting point at the city centre.

The Adelaide Parliament House (right), is viewed across the Festival Centre Plaza and part of the colourful Hajek sculpture. Although the original design of the Parliament House was not followed, and the House of Assembly and Legislative Council chambers were built 50 years apart and in different interior styles, the building, with its imposing grey frontage of Corinthian columns, remains one of the most impressive in Adelaide.

The Remarkable Rocks (following pages) at Kirkpatrick Point on Kangaroo Island are among the island's most unusual natural features. Sculptured by the winds and wild seas of the Southern Ocean, these rocks have been shaped into strange towers and a spectacular promontory.

The coastline of Kangaroo Island is wildly beautiful. Rugged headlands protect sandy bays where dramatic sand dunes (left) are formed by the pure white sands of the island. With its protected wildlife, attractive beaches and splendid scenery, the island has become a popular family holiday destination.

Abandoned stone farmhouses (opposite, bottom) are a common sight throughout South Australia. Some of these buildings are the result of changes in fashion; a new generation deserts the old house and builds a more modern dwelling. Others are reminders that life on the land is hard and takes its toll. Invariably the farmhouse stands as a stark reminder of the loneliness of Australian rural life.

For many years Kangaroo Island was the home of sealers and whalers who decimated the local animal population. Today the island's wildlife, including the sea lion (above), is protected. Sometimes known as the hair seal, the sea lion was all but wiped out by the sealers, but has recently returned to the island.

Cooper Creek (previous pages) is one of the great mysteries of outback Australia. This irregularly flowing river runs from south-western Queensland into South Australia. Here it flows into Lake Eyre, which has filled with water only twice this century. Occasionally the rains in Queensland result in the river flooding, but mostly it is little more than a collection of waterholes and dry riverbeds.

The Barossa Valley is the most famous wine-growing region in the country. The self-contained village of Seppeltsfield (above left) was established in

1851 by Joseph Seppelt, all of whose attempts to grow a variety of crops failed until he experimented with grapes. The result, by the 1890s, was one of the largest and most modern wineries in the British Empire. Today Seppeltsfield stands as a monument to the tenacity of the early grape growers.

Collingrove Homestead
(opposite, bottom), near Angaston, became the Angas family home as well as headquarters for their considerable pastoral interests. The family made their fortune raising Shorthorn cattle, and John Howard Angas was regarded

as the greatest cattle breeder of his time. Presently a National Trust property, this handsome house offers a rare opportunity to experience the lifestyle of wealthy nineteenth-century pioneers.

The Old Angaston Town Hall
(above), now the Institute/Library building, was built in 1911 and is one of the most impressive marble structures in South Australia. The marble was all quarried in the area and the building, when completed, had cost a total of £3,000. Over the years it has been used as a library, a place for town dances and a cinema.

As evening approaches and the desert starts cooling down, lengthening shadows draw the subtle designs of the desert dunes (left) into sharp relief. All over the northern two-thirds of South Australia, the desert dunes push against the roadways, rising and falling like waves. These extraordinary formations can at times reach heights of between 15 and 20 metres.

Past Port Augusta is a desert which continues to the northern half of the Northern Territory. This is the true outback, where living is hard, water is in short supply, the skies are a blinding blue, the nights cold and the days so hot that, without water, a person can die within hours. Nowhere is the landscape more isolated than beyond the tiny, one-time railway town of Innamincka (above).

NORTHERN TERRITORY

PEOPLE CALL THE NORTHERN TERRITORY 'the dead heart' or simply 'The Centre', a sparsely populated area spreading from the centre of the continent to the northern coastline, and famed for its vast tracts of uninhabited deserts. It is here that both Uluru (formerly known as Ayers Rock) and The Olgas loom out of the red desert sands, great mountains of ancient rock resisting the erosive power of intense sunshine, harsh desert winds and the climatic extremes which send temperatures soaring over 40 °C during the day and tumbling below freezing point at night. Despite this, the Northern Territory is a region of breathtaking beauty. To the north, lapped by the warm water of Van Diemen Gulf — its muddy estuaries home to crocodiles and its landscape littered with huge termite mounds — lies Kakadu National Park, the jewel of Australia. To the west of Kakadu is the equally beautiful, although lesser-known, Litchfield National Park with its clear pools and spectacular waterfalls. To the south lies the flat plateau of the Barkly Tablelands where millions of hectares of land are grazed by cattle. But the unique beauty of the Northern Territory lies around Alice Springs, affectionately called 'The Alice' by locals. It is here, under deep blue skies, that the MacDonnell Ranges spread to the east and west, their bedding twisted into fantastic shapes and the gorges and pools giving welcome relief from the heat of the surrounding desert. The red and rugged nature of these mountains is a foretaste of the beauty of Uluru.

Uluru (left), 'the greatest stone on earth', rises 348 metres above the surrounding countryside and has a circumference of 9.4 kilometres! This huge monolith, 862.5 metres above sea level, is located nearly 1,400 kilometres south of Darwin and 465 kilometres southwest of Alice Springs.

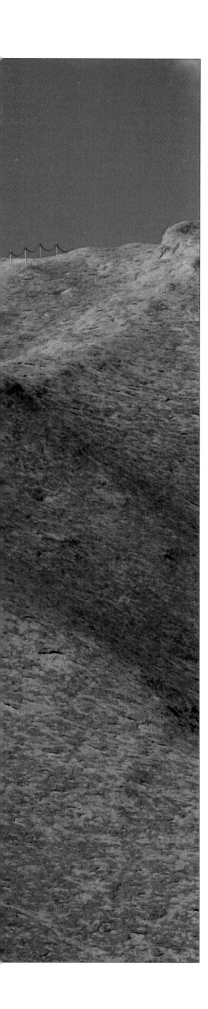

Each day hundreds of visitors climb to the top of Uluru (left). However, it does require a certain level of fitness, and the Aboriginal notion that this is a sacred site which should not be walked on, should also be respected. Although the traditional owners will never be seen climbing the rock, they have resigned themselves to the fact that visitors behave differently.

Seen from Uluru, Kata Tjuta (above), formerly called The Olgas, rewards visitors with magnificent vistas. No one is sure how these two strange formations came into existence but the most widely held theory is that both Uluru and Kata Tjuta are remnants of a vast sedimentary bed, laid down some 600 million years ago. The bed was spectacularly tilted so that Uluru now protrudes at an angle of up to 85 degrees. The rock is actually grey but is covered with a distinctive red iron oxide coating.

Those who have experienced it claim that nothing can compare with those rare moments when it rains on Uluru. Given that the rock receives on average 200-250 milli-metres of rain per annum, and that desert temperatures typically range between -8 °C at night-time in winter and 47 °C during the day in summer, visitors have to be lucky to witness rain and mist on the rock (previous pages).

The Standley Chasm (opposite) in the MacDonnell Ranges is one of the most popular attractions around Alice Springs. A 20-minute walk takes visitors right into the chasm, which is at its most spectacular at noon when the sun strikes the walls on both sides. The gorge, now owned and managed by the Angkerle Aboriginal Corporation and Iwupataka Land Trust, was named after Mrs Ida Standley, the first formal school teacher in Alice Springs and reputedly the first white woman to walk through the gorge.

The Katherine Gorge National Park (above), showpiece of the Katherine area, is a place of spectacular beauty. Katherine Gorge itself comprises 13 gorges, each of which is separated by rocky areas in the dry season. Apart from swim-ming and bushwalking, visitors can hire canoes and make their own way, at their own pace, up the gorges, or go on one of the cruises.

The Devil's Marbles Conservation Reserve lies on either side of the Stuart Highway, 10 kilometres north of Wauchope. Although geologists explain that the rocks were formed by spheroidal weathering, Aboriginal legend has it that the 'Marbles' (above), which are roughly egg-shaped, were laid by the Rainbow Serpent during the Dreamtime. Like Uluru, these remarkable boulders, some balanced precariously on others, are at their best when the rays of the setting sun catch the red iron minerals which have covered the rocks.

Alice Springs (opposite) has many drawcards for the traveller. A good starting point for any exploration is Anzac Hill, affording a superb 360° panorama of the town and environs.

The seemingly endless termite mounds (left), huge, rock-hard homes that stand as monuments to the termites which build them, are characteristic of the Barkly Tableland. At one point, in the Litchfield National Park, the mounds all point in the same direction.

The Diamond Beach Hotel Casino (above), built on the shore at Mindil Beach, is a $30-million complex designed to appeal to those who are keen to enjoy the good life while at the gambling tables. It offers luxury accommodation, fine restaurants and nightclubs.

WESTERN AUSTRALIA

WESTERN AUSTRALIA, Australia's largest state, covers nearly one-third of the continent. Mostly a desert region, the majority of the state's population, apart from the hardy miners who battle savage summer temperatures to extract iron ore and precious metals, clings to the coast. In the south and southwest, white, sandy beaches are edged by grey, granite cliffs, and chilly winds, known to locals as 'the doctor', gust in off the Southern Ocean. Around Perth, a charming, modern city which succesfully manages to mix the old and the new, the coast offers beaches ideal for swimming and fishing. To the north the red sands of the desert, and the huge sand dunes which dominate most of the eastern region of the state, come to the edge of the Indian Ocean. It is here that the famous dolphins of Monkey Mia come to the shore to welcome visitors. It is here that the isolated resort at Cable Beach, near Broome, stands alone on a seemingly endless stretch of sand, and it is here, in the wide, tropical estuaries of the north, that saltwater crocodiles sleep in the sun, waiting for their prey to enter the waters. In Western Australia the distances are so vast that the traveller can drive for a whole day and pass just one tiny township or a solitary, isolated service station.

Perth (left), the capital of Western Australia, is known for its great charm and beauty. The elegant riverside parks, the network of freeways and the languid beauty of the Swan River combine to give the city grace and distinction. Perth is the centre of the state's economic life and in recent times the skyline has risen in keeping with the fortunes of the state, particularly the mining industry.

Kings Park (opposite), also called Mount Eliza, offers a superb view of Perth and the graceful Swan River. It has been a source of pleasure to Perth residents since it was set aside as parkland in 1831 by the colony's first Surveyor General, John Septimus Roe. Named Perth Park in 1872, it was subsequently renamed Kings Park in 1901 to honour Edward VII's accession to the throne. Apart from being the one place every tourist in Perth gets to visit, the park is also popular with locals.

Since the earliest settlement visitors to Kings Park (above) have extolled its virtues. When Daisy Bates gazed from the lookout around the turn of the century she noted: 'I can never look down on the panorama of that young and lovely city from the natural parkland on the crest of Mount Eliza that is its crowning glory without a vision of the past, the dim and timeless past when a sylvan people wandered its woods untrammelled, with no care or thought for yesterday or tomorrow, or of a world other than their own. Scarcely a hundred years have passed since that symmetry of streets and suburbs was a pathless bushland, a tangle of trees and scrub and swamp with the broad blue ribbon of river running through it, widening from a thread of silver at the foot of the ranges to the estuary marshes and the sea.'

Rottnest Island (above) is Perth's favourite holiday and day-tripping destination. Only 12 minutes by air and 2 hours by water, the island is an accessible location for those wishing to escape from Perth.

The Leeuwin-Naturaliste National Park (opposite), on the coast south of Perth, is dramatically beautiful. To people who love coastal scenery, wildflower displays and untouched rugged cliffs, this park has much to offer. Winding around the Cape, either to Shelley Beach or to the area of sand dunes known mysteriously as the 'Other Side of the Moon', is a series of interesting bushwalks. The Cape also includes delights such as Lookout Rock near Castle Bay which offers superb views over Geographe Bay. In the nineteenth century it was used by sailors to spot whales swimming up the coast. Then there is Curtis Bay where a sailor, Anthony Curtis, used to load cattle onto his ship by swimming them out and pulling them aboard by their horns!

Wave Rock (left), near Hyden, is one of the many granite outcrops, formed 3,000 million years ago, which dot the Central Wheat Belt. Shaped like a huge roller about to collapse, Wave Rock is over 100 metres long. Its form was probably caused by the weathering of the rock below ground before it was exposed. The shape has been highlighted by vertical streaks of algae which grow on the surface of the 'wave' as dark stains, changing to brown in the dry season.

To the east of Perth is wheat country (above). Hundreds of towns are characterised by just a railway line, grain silos, a pub and a farm machinery sales yard. Despite the monotony of the landscape, fields of wheat symbolise productivity and enterprise.

The Pinnacles (opposite), located near the coastal town of Cervantes, are one of Western Australia's most unusual natural formations. When rains fell on the sand dunes, the water leached through the sand carrying calcium which solidified into soft limestone. No-one is certain how long this process took; it may have started as far back as 500,000 years ago, or it may be only a few thousand years old, or the process could still be continuing. The advent of drier weather in the region gradually cleared the ground of its top layer of plants and soil, exposing the pinnacles so that today they stand like strange sentinels on a plain of windblown sand.

The area around Exmouth (top) was known to Dutch sailors from the early seventeenth century. The first Europeans to sight North West Cape were Haevik Claeszoon von Hillegom and Pieter Dirkszoon, who sailed through the area in the *Zeewolf* on 24 June 1618. A month later Willem Jansz and Captain Jacobsz came ashore from their ship *Mauritius*. The ship's log recorded: 'On the 31st of July we discovered an island and went ashore, found human footsteps, on the west side the land extended NNE and SSW; it was the length of fifteen mijlen; northern extremity is in twenty-two degrees S.' What they had landed on was not an island but North West Cape.

The 260-kilometre Ningaloo Reef lies close to the shore and forms a kind of natural lagoon, ideal for people wishing to fish, snorkel, scuba dive or explore the reef — although the waters of Coral Bay (above) are a sanctuary area where 'no fishing' regulations apply. Lying just to the north of the Tropic of Capricorn, the waters are generally warm and the beaches, like most on the Western Australian coast, are white, hard and beautifully clean.

The thorny devil (above), also called the thorn devil, thorn lizard, mountain devil and the spiny agamid lizard, is a unique creature of Western Australia. Found only in the southern and western regions of the state, the reptile is covered with sharp spines from head to tail and grows to about 15 centimetres. It lives on small black ants, and has been known to eat more than 1,000 ants in a single sitting!

Western Australia can boast the longest and straightest roads in the country, with extraordinary distances between townships in the northwest and southeast of the state. The official decision to let motorists know that they should keep an eye out, not so much for pedestrians as for kangaroos, wombats and emus (right), is therefore hardly surprising!

Coral Bay (opposite) lies at the southern end of the Ningaloo Marine Park, an area that offers visitors a rare opportunity to inspect the reef and its fauna at close quarters. At points the reef is no more than 100 metres from the shore. Its waters are home to such creatures as the whale shark, the humpback whale, green turtles, dolphins and dugongs. It also boasts 170 hard corals, 11 soft corals and 475 fish species. In its own way, it is as impressive as the Great Barrier Reef.

Monkey Mia (above) is one of the true wonders of Australia (interestingly, it is pronounced as Monkey My-a and not Mee-a). In the early 1960s, a certain Mrs Watts started feeding the wild dolphins which followed her husband's fishing boat to a campsite on the shoreline. Today this feeding still occurs and Monkey Mia offers a unique opportunity for people to make contact with these mysterious sea creatures.

The Australian outback is one of the most isolated areas on earth. Often a creek, a pub or a solitary building will stand out in the middle of an area where there has been no sign of life for hundreds of kilometres. Nowhere is this more apparent than in the Kimberley area of northwestern Western Australia (previous pages). The distances are vast and lonely, the sense of isolation overwhelming.

On the vast cattle stations of northern Australia, from the Gulf to the Kimberley, the cattle range across thousands of hectares of marginal land. The challenge of the muster involves both courage and tenacity. To catch wild bullocks in a land with no fences and no roads, new mustering techniques were required (above).

Kangaroos (opposite) are the best-known of all Australian marsupials. They live on grasses and leaves, sleep during the day and feed at dusk and in the early morning. Their long tails support them and are used like a rudder when hopping. After birth, the young make their way to the mother's pouch, where they stay until they can feed themselves. Fast-moving animals, kangaroos have been recorded at speeds of up to 60 kilometres per hour.

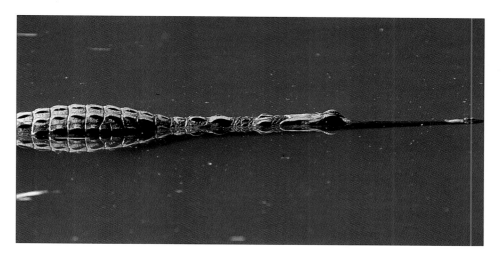

The Durack family established the vast Lissadell, Argyle, Rosewood and Ivanhoe cattle stations in the Kimberley region. It was at the Ivanhoe Station, to the north of Kununurra, that Kimberley Durack first began experimenting with the possibility of growing cash crops on the rich, black alluvial soils of the Ord River valley. This was later to evolve into the Ord River Scheme. Ivanhoe Crossing (opposite) near Kununurra was named after this famous property.

Without the assistance and talent of Aboriginal stockmen (top), the successful development of Australia's northern cattle industry would have been impossible. Widely regarded as some of the best horsemen in the world, the stockmen could deal with vast herds on difficult terrain. Recently they have applied their expertise on stations now owned and successfully run by Aboriginal cooperatives.

The freshwater crocodile (above) in Western Australia will not attack human beings, or that is what people say. Still, given the reputation of their saltwater relatives, it requires considerable courage to go swimming in the many rivers and gorges of northern Western Australia.

El Questro Station lies to the south of Wyndham in the northeast Kimberley region. The Chamberlain River (left) runs through the property, once part of the vast Durack holdings of the Kimberley region. This is hard country, which required exceptional bushcraft and tenacity to tame.

The vast region known as the Kimberley is cut by a number of gorges which are often dry for long periods. Each summer monsoonal rains, known as 'the wet', fill the streams and gorges. Over time, gorges like Cathedral Gorge (right) cut through the rock strata, creating beautiful formations.

The Bungle Bungles (previous pages), known to the local Aborigines as Purnululu, are one of the wonders of outback Australia. They would certainly be a premier tourist attraction if they weren't so inaccessible. Formed over 350 million years ago, the sandstone massif looks like a series of gigantic, bell-shaped rock towers. The horizontal banding is produced by layers of black lichens and orange silica. The sandstone is so fine that it crumbles when touched. The area is a wonderland of Aboriginal art, huge gullies and dramatic caves.

Windjana Gorge (left) is a narrow canyon approximately 90 metres deep and five kilometres long which has been cut through the Napier Range by the Lennard River. It is the central feature in the 2,100-hectare Winjana Gorge National Park, which is located some 150 kilometres east of Derby on a road known as one of the last remaining challenges on the journey around Australia.

The boab or baobab tree (above), with its thick trunk and stunted foliage, is a common sight when one travels the Great Northern Highway from the coastal town of Broome to Kununurra. These trees are the sentinels of the Kimberley region and the northwestern part of the Northern Territory.

Kununurra's greatest attraction, the Mirima Hidden Valley National Park, lies just two kilometres from the town centre. The waters of Lily Creek have eroded the quartz sandstone, creating the picturesque Hidden Valley (above and following page) with its strangly shaped formations.

In 1883 Patrick 'Patsy' Durack began his epic trek from southwest Queensland to the Kimberley with 7,250 head of breeding cattle and 200 horses. It was the longest overlanding of cattle ever attempted in Australia and lasted two years and four months. 1884 saw the first settlement of the East Kimberley. Out of the desperate isolation of the area, great cattle runs, including the Durack River Station with Jack's Waterhole (right), were forged.